AN INTRODUCTION TO THE L̶ ̶ ̶ ̶
DRAWING AND PAINTING

Volume I
THE PAINTER'S TERMS

BY

ARTHUR POPE
PROFESSOR OF FINE ARTS IN HARVARD UNIVERSITY

Cambridge
HARVARD UNIVERSITY PRESS
1929

PRINTED AT THE HARVARD UNIVERSITY PRESS
CAMBRIDGE, MASS., U. S. A.

PREFACE

THIS book is the first of a series which is designed to form an introduction to drawing and painting as a means of expression — in other words, as a language. The whole series might be thought of as a "rhetoric" of drawing and painting, in that it proposes to consider the general principles on which the art of drawing and painting is based. The first volume deals with the theory of tone relations, or what is ordinarily spoken of as color — that is, with the fundamental terms of all drawing and painting. The second volume will consider the different modes of drawing and painting — the different "dialects" which have been employed in the past or may be employed at the present day — and the various conventions and limitations which distinguish their use. To understand paintings made by Chinese or by Renaissance Italian artists, it is in a way just as necessary to know the conventions and points of view which governed their execution, as it is to know Chinese and Italian in order to understand books written in these languages. It is the object of this volume to make the different kinds of drawing and painting intelligible. The third volume will deal with the principles of design, especially in regard to their application to pictorial composition, and the fourth will consider the processes and procedures of drawing and painting.

The first volume is based on my earlier pamphlet called *Tone Relations in Painting*, and, like it, is borne more or less of necessity, since a revised statement of the subject-matter of that pamphlet is required for the use of students in Harvard University. To make the general subject of color or tone more understandable for other readers, a few plates in color have been added, not as standards of measure, for they are necessarily only approximate suggestions, but purely as illustrations to make the ideas as clear as possible to persons who are not actually making the various fundamental charts under supervision in classes.

In considerable part the present work naturally makes no great claim to originality. The main terminology and classification of tone relations proposed by Dr. Ross in his various books, and used for many years in courses in Harvard University, as well as in other institutions, have been followed for the most part. This classification is of course an approximation; but in working with pigment mixtures the painter is necessarily dealing with approximations, and he must have some system of classification that is easily workable. At the same time he should understand in what the limitations of his practice actually consist in order to have a complete idea of his whole problem. In this connection it has not seemed necessary to deal at length with the physics of light or the physiology and psychology of vision, for there are many books devoted to these still imperfectly understood and somewhat controversial matters, to which the reader may easily refer.[1] I have attempted, however, to show the relation of the terminology and the classification employed in this book to other terminologies and other classifications. I have also dealt with the difference between additive and subtractive mixing of color and with the difference between a true tone solid and the approximate solid which is devised here for practical use. Furthermore I have tried to show the difference between the factors of *value* and *color-intensity* (*chroma*) and the entirely distinct factors sometimes called by scientific writers *brightness* and *saturation*, for a great deal of confusion

[1] The titles of some of these books will be found in the Bibliographical Note, pages 155–157.

of thought has resulted from the failure to distinguish between these two sets of factors. For example, color-intensity (or chroma) and saturation are often treated as equivalent terms, and they may of course be so used; but saturation is often used in a sense which is not at all identical with that of color-intensity or chroma, as these two terms are ordinarily defined. There is often the same confusion in the use of the term brightness. The trouble is that it is not usually understood that there are actually two sets of factors involved instead of one set.

It may seem rather absurd at first to suggest that a painter or a student of painting, to say nothing of the general public, should spend a lot of time trying to understand the rather complicated theory of color or tone relations. But drawing and painting are visual arts and deal primarily with the terms of vision. A knowledge of these terms and of the possibilities of their arrangement in the art of drawing and painting is fundamental to a complete understanding of the subject. Ignorance in this respect is responsible for much vagueness and narrowness of point of view in criticism, and for much gushing sentimentality in what usually goes under the title of appreciation. As for practice, one may feel very sure that the great painters of the past have known fairly well what they were about. Their knowledge, however, was a matter of workshop tradition; it was acquired slowly by experimental practice, and handed on from master to apprentice for generation after generation. This empirical knowledge based on tradition has been largely lost; and the workshop method of training which fostered it cannot be recovered under present conditions, even if it should be desirable. Knowledge of a similar nature can be obtained at the present time only by means of a study of fundamental principles. There is really no reason why a prospective artist should not know something definite about the terms of the art with which he is going to express his ideas so that his painting may be conducted on an intelligent and sensible basis. There is a popular fear that knowledge may destroy originality and imagination. It has not done so in the past, for the greatest artists, although mostly not such extreme theorists as Leonardo, have yet given much careful thought to the materials and procedures and the general aims of their craft.

To-day we have the whole art of the world spread before us as a source of inspiration. When this is looked at without any understanding of the varied cultural environments or of the principles of expression involved, is it any wonder that the result is often a mere clumsy counterfeiting of the superficial aspect of some so-called primitive art, or a vague attempt to produce something that will look as startlingly strange as some of these things which we seem to admire? It takes intelligence to apply the fundamental principles to be discovered in the varied art of the past to the problems of our own time; and this must be based on understanding on the part of the artist on the one hand, and on the part of the patron on the other. It has always been intelligence on both sides of this twofold partnership of artist and patron that has produced the great art of the past, and it is only the same sort of intelligence that can produce art of genuine significance at the present day. The art of the past has been largely a matter of rather narrow tradition — a concentrated study of the use of a limited range of materials and terms. The art of the present day must inevitably be based on a broad eclecticism — a rational eclecticism, I should like to call it. For this, in painting, as in architecture, a sound theoretical basis is a necessity.

A. P.

June, 1929.

CONTENTS

CHAPTER I

DIFFERENT FACTORS IN VISUAL TONE · A WORKING TONE SOLID AND DIAGRAMS DERIVED THEREFROM FOR PRACTICAL USE IN CONNECTION WITH PAINTING

CHAPTER II

QUALIFICATIONS AND LIMITATIONS OF THE WORKING TONE SOLID · THE TRUE TONE SOLID · SATURATION AND BRIGHTNESS · TERMINOLOGY

CONTENTS

CHAPTER III

DESIGN IN TONE RELATIONS

CHAPTER IV

TONE RELATIONS IN PAINTING

CHAPTER V

SCALED PALETTES

CONTENTS

APPENDIX

THE PAINTER'S TERMS

CHAPTER I

THE DIFFERENT FACTORS IN VISUAL TONE ·
A WORKING TONE SOLID AND DIAGRAMS DE-
RIVED THEREFROM FOR PRACTICAL USE IN
CONNECTION WITH PAINTING

The Visual Image

WHEN we say that we see objects existing in space, what actually happens is that objects are projected upon the retina of the eye by rays of light travelling from the objects to the eye. This projection on the retina of the eye —the primary basis for visual experience, which has to be transformed into sensation, and then interpreted by the mind into the facts of existence, before what we think of as seeing occurs— is a two-dimensional image (the visual image) and corresponds to a cross-section of the cone of rays of light converging on the eye. It is like the image formed on the ground-glass plate of a camera. The visual image is composed of areas distinguished from each other by differences in quantity and quality of light.[1] These areas may

[1] For the whole process of vision, for which the light acts as an external stimulus, see *Colour and Colour Theories* by C. Ladd-Franklin, Harcourt, Brace & Co., 1929; and *Colour Vision* by Sir J. H. Parsons, Cambridge University Press, 1924.

3

be placed high or low, to the right or to the left in the field of vision in relation to its center; they may be large or small in relation to other areas; they may be round, or square, or oval, or some other shape — that is, they may vary in *position*, *measure*, and *shape*. These areas may also be light or dark; they may be red or yellow or green or blue, or some intermediate color, or they may be neutral gray; they may be strong in red or yellow or some other color, or they may be weak in color — grayish. In other words, if we use the term *value* to indicate the degree of lightness or darkness, the term *color* to indicate the quality due to the predominance of some one of the wave lengths which make up white light, and the term *intensity* to indicate the strength of the color as distinguished from neutrality, we may say that these areas vary in *value*, *color*, and *color-intensity*. The term *tone* may be used in a general way to include these three factors of *value*, *color*, and *intensity*; and we may say that the visual image is made up of areas varying in *tone* (that is, in *value*, *color*, and *intensity*) and arranged in different *positions*, *measures*, and *shapes*. We may define the visual image by defining the position, the measure, the shape, and the tone of each of its areas. We define the tone

4

of an area by defining its value, its color, and its intensity; or in the case of a neutral, like white or black or an intermediate gray, which is at the zero point of intensity and hence has no color, by defining its value. While colored tones are distinguished from each other by differences of value, color, and intensity, neutral tones are distinguished by differences of value only.

We might speak of the areas which make up the visual image as *visual tones,* using the term as somewhat analogous to tone in sound. They are distinguished from auditual tones in that they are produced by light waves instead of sound waves, and that they have extension in two dimensions in space instead of in time. We might say then that the visual image is made up of visual tones (or simply tones) varying in value, color, and intensity, and arranged in different positions, measures, and shapes. We may thus speak of the areas of the visual image as tones; or we may speak of the tone of an area; or we may speak of a tone of a given value, color, and intensity in the abstract, regardless of the limitation of measure, shape, and position; and we may speak of the general tonality of a group of areas, if they approach each other closely in value, color, and intensity. These uses of the

5

term tone are convenient, consistent, and, I believe, easily understood.

Other words are often used in place of those defined above, and the same words are frequently used in other meanings, often very vaguely. It must be borne in mind that it does not much matter what words we use, so long as we define them clearly and use them consistently to express the different factors involved. An explanation of some of the variations in terminology, however, will perhaps make the one used in this pamphlet more easily understood. Thus color is sometimes used in a general sense in place of tone. In this case one may speak of the color of a white or black or gray area as well as of a red or yellow one. If color is used in this general sense instead of tone, the term *hue* must be used in place of color in the more specific sense, to indicate the distinctions as between red, yellow, green, and so forth. Munsell[1] has used these terms in this way, and scientists do so quite generally. In my opinion the use of the term tone in the general sense to include the specific value, color, and intensity, is less confusing. Munsell uses the term *chroma* in place of

[1] A. H. Munsell, *A Color Notation*. George H. Ellis Co., Boston.

6

intensity to denote the strength of color. Another authority prefers *chromaticity*. *Saturation* is sometimes used in the same sense, but it is also sometimes used in a slightly different sense, as will be explained farther on. The terms *luminosity*, *brightness*, and *brilliance* are sometimes used in place of value.[1]

[1] In the Report of the Colorimetry Committee of the Optical Society of America (Leonard T. Troland, Chairman), published in the journal of the society of August, 1922, the terms, *color, brilliance, hue*, and *saturation* are recommended as a nomenclature for the psychological factors with which we are dealing, and the following definitions are given.

Color is defined as "the general name for all sensations arising from the activity of the retina of the eye and its attached mechanisms, this activity being, in nearly every case in the normal individual, a specific response to radiant energy of certain wavelengths and intensities." (Pp. 531–532.)

"Brilliance is that attribute of any color in respect of which it may be classed as equivalent to some member of a series of grays ranging between black and white." (P. 534.)

"Hue is that attribute of certain colors in respect of which they differ characteristically from the gray of the same brilliance and which permits them to be classed as reddish, yellowish, greenish, or bluish." (P. 534.)

"Saturation is that attribute of all colors possessing a hue, which determines their degree of difference from a gray of the same brilliance." (Pp. 534–535.)

In this nomenclature *saturation* is used as the equivalent of *color-intensity* as employed in this book. The difficulty with this is that the term *saturation* is frequently used by scientists in another sense as well, as is pointed out in the second chapter of this book. No reference to this other use is made in the Report of the Colorimetry Committee. It might not be surprising if artists were to reveal such a confusion of thought and terminology, but certainly physicists and psychologists ought to be above it. One way out

7

THE TERMS OF DRAWING AND PAINTING

With pigment materials spread on a flat surface such as paper or canvas, we may produce areas which, like those composing the visual image, have extension in two dimensions. We may make these areas light or dark; we may make them red or yellow, or some other color; and we may make them strong in that color, or weak,

---

would be to speak of *saturation I* and *saturation II*; at least the distinction should be made somehow.

Aside from this, the nomenclature proposed in the Report of the Colorimetry Committee is perfectly satisfactory for scientific use, where all words have to be defined explicitly when employed in a technical sense. If one thinks clearly enough, one can get used to any sort of terminology. I am sure that I could get along perfectly understandably with a group of persons who chose to substitute the terms cat, dog, and monkey for brilliance, hue, and saturation. Unfortunately, however, in connection with the arts we come in close contact with the ordinary use of words, so that if we want to make ourselves fairly easily understandable it is advisable that we adopt a terminology which departs as little as possible from that of everyday life. So I believe that the use of the term *color* to include white and black and grays is unnecessarily confusing for any terminology that is to be widely employed. In the second chapter of this book I have suggested a terminology that I think would lend itself easily to the requirements of almost all types of persons, and would lead to a more widespread understanding of the general ideas connected with "visual tone." But I have no great expectation that such a terminology will ever be generally adopted, by both scientific and artistic groups, for instance; for nowhere are people more tenacious of their established habits than in connection with the use of technical terms to which they have become accustomed.

8

or neutral gray.[1] We may give these areas different positions, different measures, and different shapes. Thus, the terms of drawing and painting are like the terms of vision — *tones* produced by pigment materials, varying in *value*, *color*, and *intensity*, and arranged in different *positions*, *measures*, and *shapes*.

In all drawing and painting we are dealing in some way with these factors. Sometimes we may consider the arrangement of these factors only from the standpoint of the significance of their arrangement in two dimensions on the flat surface. In this we take the point of view of pure design, or what might better be called pure drawing and painting. We might at the same time use shapes of areas or lines which would suggest natural objects more or less. This might be for the interest or entertainment to be derived from the suggestion of representation, or for the sake of some symbolic significance attached to the objects suggested. Or it might be that we were able to obtain a greater amount of beauty in the individual motives developed in the form of pattern by deriving them from natural forms than by trying to invent perfectly

[1] This is of course considering the matter from a practical point of view. All tone is psychologically a matter of sensation.

9

abstract motives. In this case the natural motive would be merely the starting point and would have to be adapted to the general intent of the pattern in a manner appropriate to the particular occasion. This has been done constantly by designers of brocades, textiles, pottery and similar objects, in which the primary concern has been with the interest of surface pattern. The final excellence of the drawing or painting done from such a point of view must of course depend primarily on the character of the formal arrangement of the tones on the surface, with regard to positions, measures, and shapes, and values, colors, and intensities. At the other extreme we might have an arrangement of these factors so ordered as to produce a definite expression of existence in space beyond the plane of the painting or drawing. This requires a definite organization of the spatial and tonal factors (regardless of mere surface pattern), which may have an interest in itself. In between these two extremes we may have a great variety of types, some with more emphasis on surface pattern, others with greater emphasis on illusion (though usually not without regard to surface pattern at the same time), according to the function of the particular drawing or painting. But in all cases we are dealing with arrangements of the same terms or factors, and these are the same as the terms of vision.

TONE SCALES

In order to think and talk definitely of tone relations, we must make definite classifications or scales by which we may measure the different factors or elements in a tone; so, leaving aside for the present the question of positions, measures, and shapes, let us consider the possibilities in the way of the classification of tones with regard to value, color, and intensity, and the expression of the relations of these factors by graphic diagrams. All such classifications are necessarily arbitrary, and an infinite number may be made, but the following scales published by Dr. Ross[1] are particularly useful in the actual practice of painting. These scales are of course not mathematically accurate, but must be thought of as adjusted or tempered for the convenience of the painter. To cite only one instance, the white and black of painting are not perfect white and perfect black. The best white paint or white paper absorbs a certain propor-

[1] Denman W. Ross, *A Theory of Pure Design.* Houghton Mifflin Company, 1907.

tion of the rays of light falling upon the surface of the painting, and is only relatively white; similarly the best black pigment fails to absorb all of the light falling on the surface, and is only relatively black. Further inaccuracies and limitations of these scales will be discussed later on. For the present, we may confine our attention to the scales and the diagrams connected therewith, in order to obtain a clear understanding of the opportunities which they afford for definite thought and practice in connection with tone relations.

The Scale of Values

A convenient scale of values in neutral tones may be produced, as shown in fig. 1, and also in Plate I, by starting with the limits of *white* (Wt) and *black* (Blk), then producing a *middle value* (M), to make the same contrast with both Wt and Blk, further intermediate values of *light* (Lt), half-way between Wt and M, *dark* (D), half-way between M and Blk, and the additional intermediates of *high light* (HLt), *low light* (LLt), *high dark* (HD), and *low dark* (LD).

This scale of nine values gives sufficiently small intervals for ordinary practice and can be easily executed with a fair degree of accuracy.

In water-color it may be produced with washes of charcoal gray, or other black pigment, with the paper used for Wt.

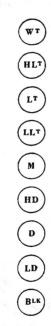

FIG. I.   The Scale of Values.

The Scale of Colors

In a similar way we may make a scale of colors, as shown in fig. 2, and in Plate II, by starting with *red* (R), *yellow* (Y), and *blue* (B), placed at equal intervals in a circular scheme. The col-

13

ors should all be produced at their highest possible intensities.[1] Intermediates of *orange* (O) to make equal contrast with both R and Y, *green* (G) half-way between Y and B, and *violet* (V) half-way between B and R, and the further in-

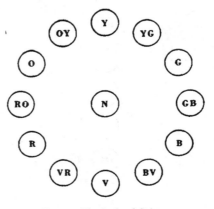

FIG. 2. The Scale of Colors.

termediates of *red-orange* (RO), *orange-yellow* (OY), *yellow-green* (YG), *green-blue* (GB), *blue-*

[1] For practical purposes the red may be considered as a color in which there is no suggestion of either orange or violet; the yellow as one which tends neither toward orange nor green; and the blue as tending neither toward green nor violet. These are purely working definitions. It must be borne in mind that this classification of colors or lines is entirely a matter of convenience in working with pigment materials, and that we are not concerned here with the process of color-vision. As is pointed out by C. Ladd-Franklin (*op. cit.*), in color-vision four primary or elementary color-sensations are involved, namely, red, yellow, green, and blue. Inter-

violet (BV), and *violet-red* (VR), may then be produced. This gives a convenient scale of twelve colors with nearly equal intervals, and approximate pigment complementaries[1]—not true complementaries — opposite, so that a line joining a pair of pigment complementaries crosses the center of the circle, where we may place *neutral* or *gray* (N.)

This scale may be produced in water-color with the following comparatively permanent pigments or mixtures of these: rose madder or alizarin crimson, vermilion, orange cadmium, aureolin or pale cadmium yellow, veridian, cobalt blue, and French ultramarine blue.

It will be noticed that in the color scale, produced in this way, the different colors at their highest intensities occur at different values. If these are compared with the value scale, it will be found that Y corresponds in value approximately to HLt, that OY and YG come approximately at Lt, O and G at LLt, RO and GB at M, R and B at HD, VR and BV at D, and V at

mediates, like orange and violet, are what she calls *color-blends* — that is, red-yellow or blue-red. In connection with the art of painting, we need not concern ourselves with these distinctions.

[1] Complementaries are any two colors which may be mixed in such a way as to produce neutral, or gray. Mixtures of pigments work on the subtractive principle and give different results from those of mixtures of light. This is explained in Chapter II.

15

LD. The colors between Y and V on the left of the circle may be spoken of in a general way as the *warm colors*, and those on the right as the *cold colors.*

The Scale of Intensities

A scale of intensities in any color may be made by starting with the limits of the color at

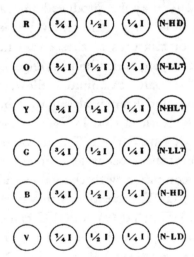

FIG. 3.   The Scale of Intensities.

highest possible intensity and the corresponding neutral of the same value, and then taking intermediates of $\frac{1}{2}$ I, $\frac{1}{4}$ I, and $\frac{3}{4}$ I, as shown for the six main colors in fig. 3 and in Plate III.

16

The degree of intensity might be expressed in another way as degree of neutralization, as shown in fig. 4.

The scales of intensities may be produced with the pigments used for the scale of colors with the addition of charcoal gray, but care must be taken to add red and orange respectively

FIG. 4. The Scale of Neutralization.

in producing the lower intensities of O and Y, in order to overcome the accidental tendency in pigment mixtures for orange to turn toward yellow, and yellow toward green, when these pigments are mixed with a black pigment.

DIAGRAMS OF VALUE AND INTENSITY FOR THE TWELVE COLORS

Diagrams expressing graphically the relations of values, colors, and intensities will be found of much assistance in achieving a clear understanding of the principles governing tone relations both in nature and in painting, and especially useful in the consideration of design in tone relations. The value and intensity possibilities of a single color may be represented as follows.

17

Let the vertical line in fig. 5 represent the scale of neutral grays from Wt to Blk. Red-orange at its highest intensity comes at the value of M, but it is distinguished from N–M by its color of red-orange and by the intensity of its color. If we measure the contrast made by RO at its fullest intensity and N–M, with the

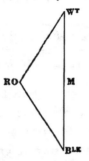

Fig. 5. The Value and Intensity Possibilities of Red-Orange.

contrast made by N–M and higher and lower values of neutral, we shall find that the contrast of RO at highest intensity and N–M about equals in attraction the contrast between N–M and N between Lt and HLt — about two and a half steps of the value scale (fig. 1). We may, then, in the diagram, place RO at its highest intensity at the same level as N–M, and at a distance from N–M laterally as shown in fig. 5 and in Plate IV. This represents with sufficient accuracy the value and intensity of RO at its great-

18

est intensity in relation to Wt and Blk and neutrals between them.

In order to raise the value of RO above M we must introduce the element of white or of some other neutral above M. If we introduce the element of white, we carry the RO toward Wt along the line from RO to Wt. In order to lower the value of RO we must introduce the element of Blk or of some other neutral below M. If we introduce the element of Blk, we move RO along the line RO to Blk. The triangle RO–Wt–Blk expresses the possibilities of the color of red-orange. We may have the color quality of red-orange at any of the values and intensities within the limits of this triangle.

We may make similar diagrams for each of the twelve colors of the color scale, as shown in fig. 6. For the sake of simplicity in the diagrams, it is arbitrarily assumed that the different colors at their greatest intensity are of equal intensity. The triangles are thus all made the same width.[1]

[1] To be perfectly accurate the triangles should be drawn of different widths. I am at present engaged in an investigation to determine the exact shapes of the different triangles, and, as nearly as possible, the shape of the true tone solid which would express the complete possibilities of value, color, and intensity for a given white light. We do not know that the outer sides of the color triangles should not be curved rather than straight lines. Troland (Report of Colorimetry Committee, p. 546) suggests a doubt as to whether the space of the tone solid is Euclidean.

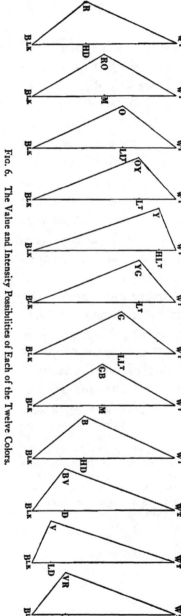

Fig. 6. The Value and Intensity Possibilities of Each of the Twelve Colors.

Notation

On each of the vertical lines in the RO triangle shown in fig. 7 there is *uniformity of intensity*. There is *uniformity of value* on each of the horizontal lines.

In fig. 8 the inclined lines from RO to Wt, and from RO to Blk, represent the highest inten-

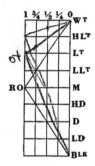

Fig. 7. Triangle of RO with Lines of Uniform Value and Uniform Intensity.

Fig. 8. Triangle of RO with Lines of Uniform Neutralization.[1]

sities of RO which can be obtained at the different value levels. The other inclined lines indicate different degrees of neutralization from the highest intensities at the different value levels.

The neutralization lines in each of the twelve triangles are shown in fig. 9.

[1] These lines have no significance except as a means of convenient notation.

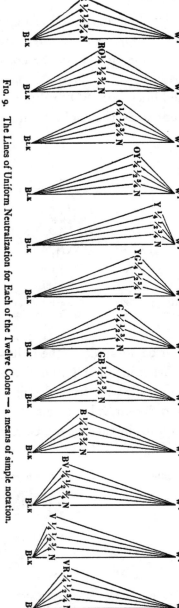

Fig. 9.   The Lines of Uniform Neutralization for Each of the Twelve Colors — a means of simple notation.

A tone may be defined either in regard to its intensity—its distance from the neutral line— or it may be defined with regard to its degree of neutralization from the highest intensity of the color obtainable at the particular value. Thus:

RO–M–$\frac{1}{4}$ I is the same as RO–M–$\frac{3}{4}$ N (neutralized).

RO–Lt–$\frac{1}{2}$ I is the same as RO–Lt (the highest intensity of RO obtainable at that value).

RO–D–$\frac{1}{4}$ I is the same as RO–D–$\frac{1}{2}$ N.

In most cases it is more convenient to define tones by their degree of neutralization, as in the second alternative shown in each case above. Thus: R–HD; R–HLt (the highest intensity of R at that value); R–M–$\frac{3}{4}$ N; O–D–$\frac{1}{4}$ N; G–Lt; G–HD–$\frac{1}{2}$ N; and so forth.[1]

The Tone Solid

A three-dimensional diagram, expressing relations of values, colors, and intensities, may be made by taking the triangles of the twelve colors and placing them so that their neutral lines coincide, forming a vertical axis from which the triangles radiate out in the order of the color

[1] Intermediate colors between any of the twelve colors in this classification might be defined as plus or minus a given color, reading the circle clockwise. Intermediate values and intensities could be distinguished in a similar manner.

circle (fig. 2). The side elevation of this three-dimensional diagram or tone solid may be constructed as shown in fig. 10.[1]

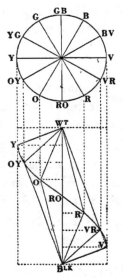

FIG. 10.   The Working Tone Solid Derived from
the Color Triangles.

A wooden model of this tone solid may be easily carved out of a cylindrical piece of wood. The colors at their fullest intensities all touch the surface of the cylinder.

[1] This is of course something like Titchener's "Colour Pyramid." See E. B. Titchener, *A Textbook of Psychology*. The Macmillan Company, N. Y.

24

This tone solid, constructed on the basis of the twelve triangles, is arbitrarily symmetrical; but it will be found very helpful as a means of getting an understanding of the main facts in connection with tone relations. The neutral line from Wt to Blk forms the axis of the solid. As we move up or down, we get changes of value; as we move outward or inward in relation to the vertical axis, we get changes of intensity; as we move around the axis, we get changes of color. At each horizontal level there is uniform value; on each radiating vertical plane, there is uniform color; on the surface of any of a series of concentric cylinders, there is approximately uniform intensity.

A chart of the twelve colors in their highest intensities at each of the seven values between Wt and Blk, as shown in fig. 11, and in plate V, gives all the main tones on the outside surface of the tone solid.

This chart may be produced in water-color with the same pigments as the scales of colors and of intensities (figs. 2 and 3) with the addition of burnt sienna to be used in making the lower values of O, OY, and Y. As in the scale of intensities, care must be taken to correct the tendency in pigments for the mixture of yellow

25

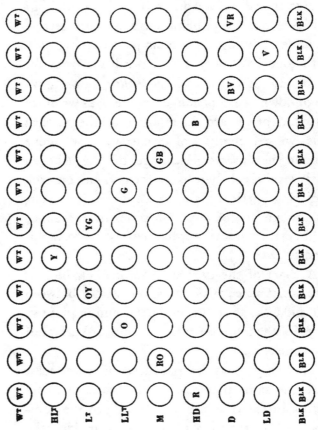

Fig. 11. Diagram of the Chart Showing the Highest Possible Intensities of the Twelve Colors at Seven Different Value Levels between White and Black.

and orange with black to produce greenish tones.

In this chart vertical rows are uniform in color, and horizontal rows are uniform in value. In connection with the horizontal sections of the tone solid, as shown in fig. 12, this chart, when carefully made, shows clearly the possibilities of color and intensity at the different value levels. At the value of HLt, Y comes at highest intensity, while OY and YG can be obtained only at considerably less intensity, O and G at still lower intensity, and the violet region, V, VR, and BV, only at very low intensities. The linear distances between the various tones in the diagram, fig. 12, express the relative strength of the contrasts between the corresponding tones in the chart, fig. 11 and Plate V. At the value of Lt, OY and YG reach highest intensity, while Y moves in toward the neutral center, and the violets and the other colors become a little more intense and, in the diagram, move out farther toward the outside of the circle. At M, RO and GB are at highest intensity, while violets and yellows are comparatively middling in intensity. Finally, at LD, the yellow region shows low intensities and limited contrasts, while violet reaches its highest intensity. The yellows and oranges in the lower values

27

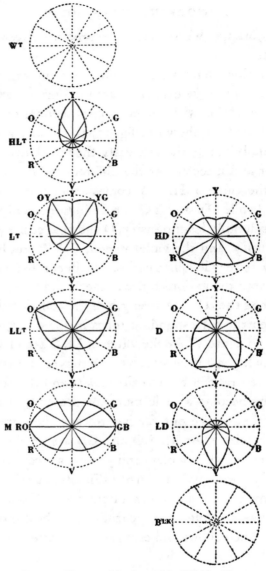

FIG. 12. Horizontal Sections of the Working Tone
Solid at the Principal Different Value Levels.

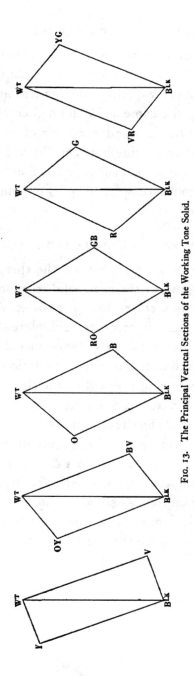

Fig. 13. The Principal Vertical Sections of the Working Tone Solid.

are what are in ordinary speech vaguely called browns, red-browns or olive-browns; but the distinctions in color quality, though less in degree, are exactly the same as in the higher values. It must be borne in mind that any color may be obtained at any value between Wt and Blk.

Vertical sections of the tone solid, as in fig. 13, show the color triangles in pairs of complementary colors.

THE DIAGRAM OF COLORS AND INTENSITIES

While it is necessary to use the three-dimensional diagram of the tone solid to express relations of values, colors, and intensities, all at the same time, and to represent complete contrasts between tones accurately, two-dimensional diagrams may be used to express relations of any two factors without regard to the third, and are very useful in actual practice.

By means of the circular plan of the tone solid, fig. 14, we may express relations of color and intensity without regard to value. This is very useful, for instance, as a basis for thinking of pigment mixtures, as shown in fig. 15.

If a red pigment is mixed with orange, the mixture falls along the line R–O—there is slight loss of the intensity of the two colors. If the R is mixed with OY, the mixture falls along the line R–OY. The half-way point is between O and RO, slightly nearer the neutral center. If the R is mixed with Y, the mixture falls along the line R–Y, and the half-way point is on the O radius, still nearer the N center. If the R is mixed with YG, the half-way point, between the Y and OY

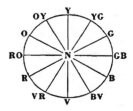

FIG. 14. Diagram of Colors and Intensities — the Plan of the Tone Solid.

FIG. 15. Diagram of Colors and Intensities, Showing Results of Mixing Pigments.

radii, is very close to the N center. Finally, if the R is mixed with G, the half-way point is N, and the other possibilities are various intensities of R and G, along the line R–N–G.

All pigment mixtures may be thought out on the basis of this diagram, so far as color and intensity possibilities are concerned. If, for example, we are painting a landscape with burnt sienna, yellow ochre, and cobalt blue, the limits of color and intensity to be obtained by this combination are explained in the diagram,

31

fig. 16. If a portrait is painted in R, Y, and N (red, yellow, and white and black pigments), as in so many portraits by the later Renaissance masters, the diagram, fig. 17, explains the limits of color and intensity to be obtained by this

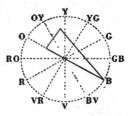

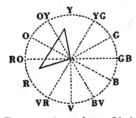

FIG. 16. Approximate Limitations of Color and Intensity Involved in the Use of Burnt Sienna, Yellow Ochre, and Cobalt Blue.

FIG. 17. Approximate Limitations of Color and Intensity Involved in much Venetian Painting.

combination. In this case the N tells in the painting as relative blue.

THE DIAGRAM OF VALUES AND INTENSITIES

A vertical diagram to express relations of value and intensity may be made by conceiving the different color triangles to be turned into the same plane around the neutral axis, and arranged right and left of this axis, as shown in fig. 18. Individual tones may be plotted at different levels to show value, and at different distances right and left of the neutral line to show intensity, as in fig. 19. Lines joining these tones in the diagram indicate the approximate contrasts between the different tones. This diagram is useful in many ways. For example, it helps to explain the general principle governing the changes of tone as objects model from light to

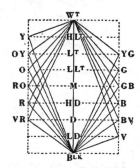

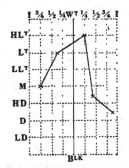

FIG. 18. Diagram of Values and Intensities.

FIG. 19. Diagram of Values and Intensities with an Indication of Relative Contrasts.

dark in nature. Suppose that in relation to the limits of light and dark in Wt and Blk, three objects, R, OY, and GB in color, have their values and intensities expressed in the diagram as in fig. 20. In the plane of light, their relative contrasts will be indicated by the line, R–OY–GB. As the objects model into shadow, the local tones become darker and also less intense in proportion. In half light they are reduced, let us say, one third toward blackness. In the diagram they

33

may be indicated by the positions, R′, OY′, GB′, and their contrasts by the line connecting them. If in the plane of shadow they are reduced two thirds toward blackness, they will be indicated in the diagram by R″, OY″, GB″. Below the plane of shadow there are possibilities of deeper

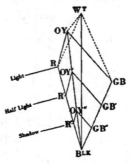

FIG. 20. Diagram of Values and Intensities Showing Proportional Diminution of Contrasts as Objects Model from Light into Shadow.

FIG. 21. Diagram of Values and Intensities Showing Modelling Scheme in much Renaissance Painting.

shadows all the way down to black, and there are possible transitional tones between the different main planes. These will all fall along the diagonal lines, R–Blk, OY–Blk, or GB–Blk. High reflected lights will, if the light is white, be plotted somewhere along the dotted lines up to Wt. This diagram expresses the general principle of proportional diminution of contrasts of values and intensities, as objects model from light into shadow.

34

By a similar diagram the actual practice of most of the mediaeval and earlier Renaissance masters may also be shown. These painters were in the habit of expressing the form of individual objects with little regard for general light effect, by modelling each field in different values without regard to the diminution of intensities in nature. A red drapery, for example, modelled according to the prescription of Cennino Cennini,[1] would be plotted as in fig. 21. The intensity is lower in the plane of light than in the plane of shadow, just the reverse of nature's principle. This was appropriate, however, for the mode of painting employed by these painters.

The Diagram of Values and Colors

A diagram expressing relations of values and colors, without regard to intensity, consists of the various triangles of the tone solid projected upon the surface of the enclosing cylinder, and unfolded on a flat plane, as in fig. 22. In this figure the triangles are each represented by a vertical line, as if seen edge on. This diagram will be found especially useful in plotting tones from the standpoint of design. By indicating the

[1] *The Book of the Art*, translated by Christina D. Herringham. London, 1899.

35

degree of neutralization with figures, as in fig. 23, a complete score of a composition may be easily

	N	R	RO	O	OY	Y	YG	G	GB	B	BV	V	VR
Wt	.	.	.	.	.	.	.	.	.	.	.	.	.
HLt	.	.	.	.	.	Y	.	.	.	.	.	.	.
Lt	.	.	.	O	OY	.	YG	.	.	.	.	.	.
LLt	.	.	O	.	.	.	G	.	.	.	.	.	.
M	.	RO	.	.	.	.	.	GB	.	.	.	.	.
HD	R	.	.	.	.	.	.	B	.	.	.	.	.
D	.	.	.	.	.	.	.	.	BV	.	VR		
LD	.	.	.	.	.	.	.	.	.	V	.		
Blk	.	.	.	.	.	.	.	.	.	.	.	.	.

Fig. 22. Diagram of Values and Colors.

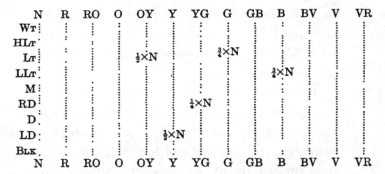

Fig. 23. Diagram of Values and Colors with Plotting of Specific Tones

recorded.[1] This diagram corresponds to the chart shown in Plate V and in fig. 11.

[1] Compare Munsell, *A Color Notation*, pp. 55–61.

CHAPTER II

ADDITIVE AND SUBTRACTIVE MIXING OF COLORS

THE impossibility of producing perfect tone
scales in pigment materials was referred to
in the last chapter. It was also stated that the
scales and diagrams there set forth were made
deliberately more or less inaccurate for the sake
of the convenience of the painter. In this one is
perhaps somewhat justified by the analogy of
the tempered scale of the pianoforte, which is
likewise conveniently inaccurate; only our scales
are rather more violently tempered.

The principal difficulty in the way of making
tone scales, which shall combine convenience for
the painter with scientific accuracy, lies in the
fact that the mixture of colored pigments gives
results frequently quite different from those obtained by the mixture of colored light. Thus,
when we mix yellow and blue pigments, the result is a greenish tone; and when we mix yellow
and violet pigments, the result is a neutral. On

37

the other hand, when we mix a yellow stream of light and a violet stream of light, the result is a reddish or orange tone; and when we mix yellow light and blue light, the result is neutral instead of green. This is due to the fact that there are two different methods of mixing colors. These are known as the additive and subtractive methods respectively, and they may be explained as follows.

Suppose that we have two lanterns throwing streams of white light on the screen at C, in fig. 25, and suppose that we place a yellow screen in lantern A and a blue screen in lantern B. We may also suppose, for the sake of simplicity, that white or neutral light is composed of a mixture of R, O, Y, G, B, and V rays. The particular color or hue of light reflected by a pigment is of course due to the fact that the pigment material has the power of absorbing certain of the wave lengths of white light and of reflecting or transmitting others. The particular color is that of the dominant wave length among those reflected; but in addition to the dominant wave length adjacent wave lengths covering a considerable portion of the spectrum are ordinarily reflected. The "spread" over the spectrum of some of the common pigment materials is shown in the diagram of relative wave lengths and energy from Luckiesh given in fig. 24.[1]

Let us suppose that the yellow pigment in the screen of lantern A in fig. 25 has the power of absorbing the B and V rays out of the white

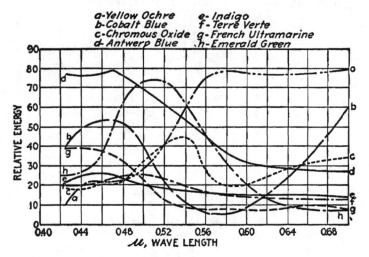

a-Yellow Ochre   e- Indigo
b-Cobalt Blue   f- Terre Verte
c-Chromous Oxide   g- French Ultramarine
d- Antwerp Blue   h- Emerald Green

FIG. 24. Spectral Analyses of Pigments.

light, and of transmitting the rest, namely the R, O, Y, and G, among which the Y is dominant; and that the blue pigment, on the other hand, absorbs the R, O, and Y, and transmits the G, B, and V, among which the blue is domi-

[1] M. Luckiesh, *Color and its Application*, fig. 122, p. 298. D. Van Nostrand Co., N. Y., 1915.

nant. If we add the two streams together, we
have all the component elements of white light
in the resulting mixture, and the mixture is neutral, as shown in fig. 25.

On the other hand, if we shut off lantern B
and put both the Y and the B screens in lantern

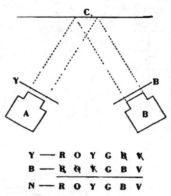

Y — R O Y G R K
B — R K K G B V
N — R O Y G B V

FIG. 25.   Additive Mixing of Color.

A, part of the rays of white light are absorbed by
the Y, and still more by the B, leaving only the
G transmitted to the screen, as shown in fig. 26.
If we should put in also a red screen, this would
absorb the G rays, and no light of any kind
would be transmitted to the screen at C. In
other words the result of the mixture would be
black.

These are of course only approximate dia-

40

grams. In fig. 27 the possible mixture of Y and a
light complementary B is indicated in a diagram
in which relative wave lengths (μ) are shown

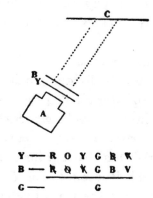

```
Y — R O Y G B V
B — R O Y G B V
C —           C
```

FIG. 26.   Subtractive Mixing of Color.

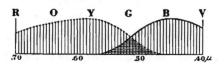

FIG. 27.   Diagram of Relative Energy and Relative
Wave Length.

Continuous line indicates reflecting power of a possible
B pigment for all wave lengths (μ). Dotted line indicates
reflecting power of a possible Y pigment for all wave
lengths. Result of additive method is shown by vertical
shading. Result of subtractive method is shown by horizontal shading.

horizontally and relative energy vertically. This
shows the "spread" of the light reflected by
each pigment material over the spectrum. Practically all pigment materials reflect a consider-

able range of wave lengths in addition to the dominant wave length which gives the particular color. The spectral distribution of the light reflected by various pigments is shown in diagrams given by Luckiesh [1] and also by Martin and Gamble.[2]

Pigments mix approximately on the subtractive principle. Finely divided particles of different colors are so intermingled that light travels perhaps first through a yellow particle and then through a blue particle, even several times over, before being reflected back from the surface of the painting. This accounts for the fact that there is always some lowering of value when pigments are mixed together, though at times it is so slight as to make no appreciable difference. The stronger the intensities and the greater the color interval, the greater will be the lowering of value in the mixture. It is partly for this reason that it is wise to avoid too intimate a mixing of the tones on the palette in actual painting.[3]

In the "color-top," or the Clerk–Maxwell discs, on the other hand, the mixture conforms to the additive principle. Owing to the phenom-

[1] *Op. cit.*
[2] *Colour and Methods of Colour Reproduction.* D. Van Nostrand Co., N. Y., 1923.
[3] See Luckiesh, *op. cit.*, pp. 297–301, and figs. 122–124.

enon known as persistence of vision, the alternating streams of Y and B falling on the retina of the eye produce much the same effect as in the case of the streams from the two lanterns in fig. 25.

When the tones in a painting are juxtaposed in the "pointillist" fashion, instead of being mixed on the palette or on the brush in the ordinary way, there is a more or less close approach to mixture of streams of light on the additive principle, as in rotation, when the picture is looked at from a considerable distance.[1] It is seldom that a painting can be satisfactorily handled completely in this manner, but there is often some compromise between mixture by addition and mixture by subtraction.[2]

[1] Lumière color photography is based on this principle.

[2] In painting one does not ordinarily have to pay much attention to the matter of additive mixing, for, except for a slight amount of additive mixing in the use of broken color, or possibly a good deal in the unusual use of an extreme method of "pointillism," pigment mixtures work on the subtractive basis; but in all work on the stage one is dealing constantly with additive as well as subtractive mixing of color. When, for example, light of different colors from two or more light sources is thrown on a plaster dome or a cyclorama, the overlapping of the streams of light of different colors results in an additive mixing. There is a certain amount of additive mixing whenever streams of light from different sources overlap on any of the objects on the stage. But there is also usually a good deal of subtractive mixing mingled with this. The pigments or dyes used in the gelatine screens which are placed in the various light sources are all subtractive agents; so are all the

Munsell worked out a color scale on the principle of rotation. This consists of five colors taken at equal intervals, as in fig. 28. When equal areas of these five colors at the same value and at the same intensity are rotated, as in the

FIG. 28.   Scale of Five Colors, Based on Additive Mixing, like that of Munsell.

Munsell sphere, they produce neutral. They are at exactly equal intervals for mixture on the additive principle.

pigment materials used in painting the scenery and dyeing the costumes. So when a colored light falls on a costume other than white, the resulting tone is a matter of subtractive mixing — a part of the white light is absorbed by the screen and still more by the pigment material in the costume. For instance, the usual amber screen used in stage lighting absorbs all the blue region of the spectrum; so when amber light is thrown on a blue dress the latter looks gray or black — it cannot reflect any blue unless there is some blue in the light coming to it, and there is no blue in this case. The changes in value as well as color and intensity are sometimes very startling, as the tone of the light is changed; often they are quite inexplicable to the person who knows nothing of color theory. The lighting man on the stage must know something of the spectral composition of the dyes in his gelatine screens, and also of the pigments used in the painting of the scenery and the dyes used in the costumes, before he can tell even approximately what effect his lights are going to produce.

44

In the tone solid shown in the last chapter the intervals between the colors correspond approximately to pigment mixtures; approximate pigment complementaries — not true complementaries — are placed in opposing pairs.

FURTHER LIMITATIONS OF THE WORKING TONE SOLID

A marked defect in the tone solid shown in the last chapter lies in the fact that the triangles of the twelve colors are made all the same width, although the colors produced at the highest intensities obtainable with our pigment materials are not all of the same intensity. The RO of our color scale is much more intense than the GB, for example. In order to make a tone solid which would express intensity relations accurately, it would be necessary to vary the width of the triangles according to the relative contrasts of intensities and values. This would produce an irregular instead of a symmetrical solid.

This difficulty is avoided in Munsell's sphere by placing what he calls No. 5 chromas (exactly uniform intensities) on the equator of the sphere, all the same distance from the neutral axis. There is an error in this, however, in that the relation between intensity (or chroma) contrasts and value contrasts is not observed. Consequently in Munsell's diagrams showing the highest intensities (chromas) of the different colors, these are placed at great distances from the neutral axis, indicating, for instance, a contrast between R at its highest intensity and N of the same value greater than the contrast between Wt and Blk. As a matter of fact, the latter

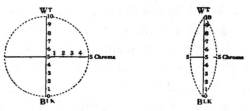

Fig. 29. Diagrams Illustrating Partial Inaccuracy of
Munsell Color Sphere.

contrast is much greater, and the Munsell sphere and other solids and diagrams are not thoroughly accurate in this respect. The sphere, to be perfectly accurate, ought to be a bobbin-shaped figure of smaller diameter, approximately as indicated in fig. 29.

A fact to be noted in connection with the Munsell charts is that they are based on tones produced with opaque pigments, and higher intensities may be produced in transparent pigments than in opaque pigments. The highest

46

intensities come at different value levels when produced with transparent pigments. On the other hand, they do not correspond exactly to the values of the value scale, as would be indicated by the symmetrical tone solid. The highest intensity of V, for example, comes considerably above LD, though possibly the greatest purity or saturation of V may be obtained at about that value (see farther on in this chapter), and G is probably placed at somewhat too high a value. This is a further inaccuracy of the symmetrical tone solid; nevertheless in a general way the steady descent of the high intensity line from Y to V, through either the warm or the cold colors, would probably be a feature of the true tone solid.

In spite of the limitations noted above, the symmetrical tone solid and the scales derived from it are most convenient devices to be used as aids to definite thinking about tone relations. The scales are easily produced, and even memorized, with approximate accuracy, so that a painter, indeed anyone, may very quickly make use of them and the various diagrams connected with them almost unconsciously.

A True Tone Solid

It has been pointed out above that the symmetrical tone solid shown in the last chapter is only an inaccurate approximation devised for practical purposes. By plotting out the relations of values and intensities to be obtained from a given set of pigments, this could be made perfectly accurate by working along the line of a variation of the Munsell solid. The color intervals would have to be shifted to conform with the principle of additive mixing — that is, to give accurate visual intervals. Such a solid would be irregular in shape.

The complete content of tone in a given strength of white light would of course have to be shown in a more extended diagram, for complete possibilities of tone cannot be achieved in paint. White pigment, for example, always absorbs a certain amount of the light falling on its surface, and is not usually more than about 80 per cent perfect. In a similar way black pigment is never perfect black, but always reflects a certain amount of light that falls on its surface. A true tone solid would show the complete possibilities of value, color, and intensity for a standard white light.

48

It is assumed that the color-intensities in such a tone solid would be plotted by a comparison of the different colored tones with neutral grays. It is a well-known fact that colors may be made, by inference, to appear more intense than this by juxtaposing them to other colors — especially their visual complementaries. Therefore to make a tone solid that would be entirely inclusive of all color-intensities within the limits of possible visual sensation, it would be necessary to enlarge the solid described above in the dimension of color-intensity to take in all color-intensities that could be achieved in this way.

The Distinct Factors of Saturation and Brightness

One difficulty that has constantly produced confusion of thought as well as of terminology in connection with the general consideration of tone or color has been the constant failure on the part of both physicists and psychologists to distinguish between the factor which I have called color-intensity—and is by Munsell called chroma—and a different factor which is usually called purity or saturation; and to distinguish also between what I have here called value and a different factor which is sometimes called brightness.

49

In order to define any tone accurately from the visual or psychological point of view, it is only necessary to state its color and value and color-intensity (chroma);[1] but the two further factors, which I shall call *saturation* and *brightness*, must be considered if one is to possess a complete understanding of the subject. As a matter of fact a tone could be defined by stating its relative color, brightness, and saturation, instead of its color, value, and intensity, and this method of classification has been sometimes used.[2] It is necessary to distinguish clearly between these two systems of classification and the factors involved in each of them, for this is not, as has often been supposed, merely a matter of the use of equivalent terms for the same factors.

Let us suppose that we have a pigment which when spread over a flat surface gives us the

[1] By value is meant the degree of lightness or darkness of the tone in relation to the limits of white and black.

By color is meant the specific quality of the tone due to the dominance of one of the wave lengths of all those which combined produce white.

By color-intensity or chroma is meant the strength of the color-factor in the tone — in other words its distinguishability from neutral of the same value.

[2] This method has apparently been used by Ruxton. See Martin and Gamble, *op. cit.*, p. 30, and Luckiesch, *op. cit.*, pp. 82–84.

50

color of orange; that this pigment is, for the sake of simplification of argument, of such a quality that it reflects perfectly all orange wave lengths out of white light which falls upon the painted surface, but that it absorbs all of the other wave lengths. We have then orange of absolute purity,

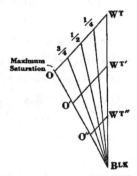

FIG. 30.   Diagram of Value and Intensity Possibilities of Orange,
Showing Lines of Uniform Relative Saturation.

and also of highest possible energy for this particular wave length. In a diagram of values and intensities, as in fig. 30, in which the white and black are assumed to be perfect white and perfect black, the orange sensation produced by this perfect orange pigment, being of highest possible intensity or chroma for this particular color,[1] will come, let us suppose, at O. If the

[1] This is probable—at any rate the assumption is near enough the truth for present purposes.

strength of the illumination on the painting surface is lowered until the white is lowered to Wt′,
the orange will be reduced to O′. If the illumination is lowered still farther until white comes
at Wt″, the orange will fall to O″ in fig. 30. It
is possible that these changes in tone might also
be achieved by changes in the quality of the pigment — that is, if we could add a perfect black
pigment to the orange. If we call the common
visual quality in the different tones along the line
O–Blk in fig. 30 *saturation*, we may say that all
the tones along the line O–Blk are of uniform
saturation, and of uniform maximum saturation.
White added to the orange would diminish its
saturation along the line O–Wt. If a scale of
relative saturation were measured along this line,
the diagonal lines between the line O–Blk and
the line Wt–Blk would be lines of uniform relative saturation, as shown in fig. 30.

The orange pigment assumed in the above is
supposed to reflect the orange wave length at its
full strength or energy. As the orange is carried
along the line O–Wt, more and more of the energy of the other wave lengths of white light is
added to the orange, but the full strength or
energy of the orange wave length remains as a
component element in the tones all the way to

white. If we call the common visual quality in the different tones along the line O–Wt, due to the presence of the full energy of the orange wave length in all these tones, *brightness*, we may say that all the tones along the line O–Wt are of uniform brightness, and of uniform maximum

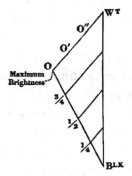

FIG. 31. Lines of Uniform Relative Brightness of Orange.

brightness. If a scale of relative brightness is measured along the line O–Blk, lines drawn from the various points of this scale to the neutral line Wt–Blk parallel to the line O–Wt will be lines of uniform relative brightness, like the lines O'–Wt' and O''–Wt'' in fig. 30, or the lines of $\frac{1}{4}$, $\frac{1}{2}$, and $\frac{3}{4}$ brightness in fig. 31.

Now let us turn for a moment to the treatment of the matter of saturation and brightness in one or two scientific books. In *Color and Its*

Application by Luckiesh, on page 80, the term saturation is used as the equivalent of Munsell's chroma and our term intensity; but on page 71 it is used in the entirely different sense which I have defined above. Luckiesh writes:

"On diluting a color with white light, tints are obtained; that is, tints are unsaturated colors. By the admixture of black to a color (in effect the same as reducing the intensity of illumination) the brightness is diminished without altering either the hue or the saturation, and various shades are produced."

The "tints," in our diagram in fig. 30, would come on the line O–Wt, and the "shades," obtained by the "admixture of black . . . without altering . . . the saturation" would come on the line O–Blk; and on this line there is steady "alteration" of chroma or color-intensity all the way to Blk. This is, I believe, a perfectly proper sense in which to use the term saturation; but if it is used in this sense, it must not be supposed that it is equivalent to chroma or color-intensity.[1]

To take another example, in *Colour and Meth-*

[1] It seems clear that the term *saturation* should either be used in a sense distinct from that of *color-intensity* or *chroma*, or else, as suggested above, a distinction should be made between *saturation I* and *saturation II*.

54

ods of Colour Reproduction by Martin and Gamble, on page 12, saturation, purity, and chroma are grouped together as equivalent terms; but on page 30 is the following passage referring to the Ruxton classification of tones or colors:

"Each spectral hue is shown in three saturations [the two weaker saturations are de-

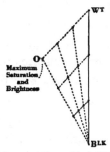

FIG. 32.   Relative Values and Intensities of Tones in a Classification Based on Saturation and Brightness.

scribed in this case as being made by mixing white with the pigment at highest saturation], and each saturation is shown in three degrees of brightness (the diminution of 'value' being secured by the addition of black)."

In the case of orange the tones obtained by this arrangement would be placed on the diagram of values and intensities as shown in fig. 32.

Here both the terms brightness and saturation are used in the special sense in which I have de-

55

fined them above. They are also used in this same sense in the following passage from Martin and Gamble:

"Having formed the conception of a pure hue (which may or may not be found quite ideally in the spectrum), we may now conceive a wide range of perceptibly differing colours formed from it, for we might proceed to dilute the hue with differing amounts of white (keeping the total light always to a standard intensity) and thus form a *tint* series or series of differing saturation. Further, with any number of the same series the 'brightness' may be varied from zero upwards in a great number of perceptible steps until a 'dazzling' brightness is reached. This produces a series of *shades* of a pure hue." (Page 12.)

In another passage on the same page brightness is defined as follows:

"The brightness of coloured light may be assumed to consist generally of two parts: (1) the brightness of the component which also causes the pure sensation of hue, and (2) the brightness of any white sensation which may be present."

Just before this sentence is the following:

"The saturation, purity, or chroma of a colour refers to the proportion of the brightness of the pure hue sensation to the total brightness of the colour."

Chroma is here used as equivalent to saturation, and no allowance is made for the use of chroma in the sense in which it is defined by Munsell or for any other word to indicate what we have spoken of as color-intensity, which is the exact equivalent of Munsell's *chroma*.

Titchener[1] on the other hand uses saturation as the equivalent of chroma according to the Munsell definition. Troland's[2] use of the term saturation in this sense has already been cited (p. 7, footnote). Neither of them seems to distinguish the factor which we have called saturation, although the general consideration of this as a distinct factor would seem to warrant some consideration.[3]

The difficulty is that Martin and Gamble, along with Luckiesh and many other scientific authorities, have failed to see that in this sense

[1] E. B. Titchener, *A Textbook of Psychology*. The Macmillan Company, N. Y.

[2] *Op. cit.*

[3] In conversation Professor Troland has suggested that the co-ordinates of value (brilliance) and chroma or intensity (saturation) should be considered fundamental, and the lines of saturation and brightness, as specially defined above, two of any number of sets of lines, more or less significant according to circumstances, which might be drawn through the tone solid.

saturation and brightness, as defined above, are distinct from the factors of value and chroma or color-intensity. As shown in the accompanying diagrams, the lines of uniform relative saturation and brightness cut diagonally across the lines representing uniformity of value and of chroma or color-intensity, which are horizontal and vertical, respectively.

As a matter of fact, the term purity could be used in a different sense from saturation and chroma or color-intensity to indicate a possible isolation of a single wave length; but the significance of this from the standpoint of design, except as it affects saturation, is problematical and probably merely academic.[1] Saturation, however, has definite visual and design significance, and so also has brightness. There is a uniformity of quality in the tones along the line O–Blk which can be appreciated visually even when this is only approximated by pigment mixtures. There is a similar uniformity of quality in the tones along the line O–Wt, and this is also appreciable in the approximations of pigment mixtures. In other words, there is a uniformity of

[1] As a matter of fact *purity* in this sense would have significance only from the point of view of physics. *Saturation* and *brightness*, on the other hand, are visual or psychological qualities of tone.

brightness in all the tones on the upper surface of the tone solid. This is illustrated roughly in Plate V, where all the upper tones in each vertical row are obtained by mixing the full intensity of each color with white. These tones are what are sometimes referred to as *tints*,[1] as in the passage quoted from Luckiesh. In much of the painting of the so-called Impressionists, like Monet, Renoir, and Dodge MacKnight, the tones employed are confined to the upper surface of the tone solid. Thus there is in their works a harmony of highest possible brightness; each color, being either at highest possible intensity or else mixed only with white, is maintained, as nearly as is possible in pigment materials, at the strength of illumination which it possesses as a component of the white light falling on the surface of the painting. As a hypothesis which seems to work in actual practice, I believe that this accounts principally for the feeling of brilliant and harmonious light in the works of these painters. As explained in the discussion of the use of limited palettes in the next volume, the transposition into the Monet or MacKnight

[1] The extended use of classifications which discriminate between *tints* and *shades* is, I believe, an indication of the fact that there are common qualities in uniform brightnesses and uniform saturations which are visually appreciable.

palette is a perfectly arbitrary artistic device, and not a matter of mere breaking up of white light into its spectral components, according to the explanation frequently given.

All this discussion seems unnecessarily technical and complicated for a book on the art of painting; but where there is so much confusion of thought, it seems sensible, if it is possible, to clarify our ideas. I think it is not improbable that the treatment of saturation and brightness as separate factors, distinct from value and color-intensity, may throw some further light on the very complex subject of design in tone relations. This is dealt with briefly in the next chapter; but so far there has not been enough experimentation to determine whether the possibility has any real significance or not.

Note on Terminology

As has been indicated above, there is considerable confusion in present terminologies dealing with the general matter of what is ordinarily spoken of as color; and the one used in this book, although it is retained here because it has become more or less established in the courses in Harvard University, is not as convenient for general use as it might be made. I should like, therefore, to make the following suggestions for a somewhat different terminology, which would be more easily adaptable both to scientific and to everyday usage.

For all visual sensations we would use the term *visual tone* or *tone*.

For differences of lightness or darkness, represented by different levels in the tone solid, we would use the term *value*.

For differences as between red, green, blue, and so forth, we would use the term *hue*.

For differences in the strength of a particular hue, as compared with a gray of the same value, we would use the term *intensity* (the equivalent of *chroma* as defined by Munsell).

Then we might distinguish between those tones which are zero in intensity and hence lacking in the factor of hue, and those tones which are of a definite hue and intensity, by calling the first *neutral tones*, *uncolored tones*, *achromatic tones*, or simply *neutrals*, including the extremes of white and black and their intermediates which would be called grays; and by calling the other tones *colored tones*, *chromatic tones*, or simply *colors*.

Then *saturation* could be used in the specific sense defined above, that is, for the quality of a given tone when its hue seems undiluted by any white or gray or other tone above black; for the carrying of the tone down toward theoretical black does not dilute the hue, but merely diminishes its force.

Brightness could also be used in the sense defined above, that is, for the full force of the particular hue in a given tone — its total distance from absolute black.

Relative saturation would be determined by the degree of dilution with the neutral of corresponding brightness. *Relative brightness* would be a matter of degree of diminution of the force of the particular hue from its full force for the particular white light.

This terminology allows for the use of the terms saturation and brightness as they are actually used now in many scientific works, and it allows for the distinction between these factors and the different factors of value and intensity. Furthermore it makes it possible to use the term color in its everyday sense to include all the tones except white and black and the intermediate grays. In other words, it comes very close to the present use of terms by laymen, psychologists, and physicists.

It is of course foolish to place too much emphasis on mere nomenclature; but in a subject in which, as we have seen above, there is so much confusion of thought even among scientists, a clear and easily understood terminology that comes as close as possible to prevailing usage may be of real service.

CHAPTER III

DESIGN IN TONE RELATIONS

INTRODUCTORY

THAT all design is fundamentally a matter of order or organization of some sort is fairly generally accepted. Elsewhere [1] I have attempted to show that aesthetic experience is a question of reaction to emotionally, as opposed to intellectually, appreciable order, and that the relative value of different aesthetic experiences depends on the quantity and perfection of this appreciable order; also that two things are ordinarily necessary for this emotional experience: first, definite order or organization, and secondly, some element of contrast, of novelty, of surprise, of disorder, in fact, which at the moment does not strike one as a dominant factor, but which serves as a means to emphasize the elements of order, and without which the order would seem obvious or monotonous, and uninteresting. The exact amount of contrast or variety necessary can ordinarily be predicted only rather vaguely, but the matter of organization, at least in simpler examples, is perfectly tangible: we can be

[1] *Art Studies*, III, 133. Harvard University Press, 1925.

fairly definite about that, and approximately accurate in any given circumstance about the requirement of contrast or variety.

In applying this to the matter of tone relations we come upon one of the most difficult problems in the whole realm of the arts, and one which is very imperfectly understood. In general, persons who have what we think of as good taste are apt to agree fairly well in the face of specific examples as to what is "good color" and what is "bad color," although the effect on their taste of changing fashions and habits must always be discounted. On the other hand, when it comes to the reasons for these judgments, the ordinary explanations or prescriptions are not very satisfactory.

It has often been thought that there must be some virtue in certain intervals of color, as there is mathematical harmony in certain relations of intervals in sound; and all sorts of theories of color, even including major and minor chords, have been worked out on a basis of the most superficial analogies with musical harmony. As a matter of fact, although the same general principles of design apply to arrangements of both sound tones and visual tones, the specific application is entirely different; for sound tones not only have extension in time instead of in space, but they are distinguished as separate tones when they are overlapped—that is, played at the same time; whereas visual tones, which have extension in two-dimensional space, are destroyed by overlapping and give way to entirely new ones. The juxtaposition of tones in painting involves an entirely different application of the principles of design from what we find in music.

Most books that have been written on the subject of design indicate a failure to appreciate the complexities of the subject of tone or color design; they seem to imply that one or two simple rules might be evolved which would solve the whole problem. Thus certain writers emphasize the possible harmony to be derived from the use of low intensities of color; others emphasize the possible dominance of one color region with perhaps the use of small amounts of complementary colors to afford relief or stimulate interest. Still others suggest that all good tone design depends on a balancing of colors and intensities around a neutral center, as if in a satisfactory composition all the tones would average on neutral if they could be spun in proper proportions on a color top. This method has actually been suggested as a means of ensuring good tone de-

sign, as if this were the whole thing. One does
not have to look far to find splendid examples of
tone design which do not average on neutral at
all, but which obviously illustrate other methods
of achieving tone harmony. As a matter of fact
there are a great many different ways of achieving ordered arrangement in the tones of a composition, and of maintaining at the same time the
necessary contrast or disharmony to make this
interesting — that is, emotionally appreciable.
These possibilities may be used singly or perhaps
in combination according to circumstance.

It is proposed in this chapter to indicate
briefly the principal possibilities in the way of
ordered arrangement of the different tonal factors
of value, color, and intensity — not to suggest
them as rules that must be used in good tone
design, but as methods that may be used according to circumstance. In practice it is a very complicated affair, for not only are we often satisfied
with an approximation to a definite harmony of
tone, as long as we can feel the intention clearly,
but often the tonal arrangement of a composition has to be bent deliberately to the exigencies
of spatial design or of expression, in which case
the final organization is so complex that it may
defy exact analysis in any of its parts. Further-

more there are, I believe, possibilities in the way of tone harmony that are not yet fully understood. I cannot help having a suspicion that there are certain principles underlying the elaborate methods of dyeing used by the Persian carpet makers that account for something of the beauty of tone in the final designs, but about which we are still entirely ignorant from the theoretical point of view. Toward the end of the chapter there will be found some suggestions in regard to harmony obtained by uniformity of attraction and by uniformity of color and intensity contrast which have, I believe, not been made before except partially in my pamphlet, *Tone Relations in Painting*. Further investigation will be necessary before we may have anything like a complete understanding of the subject.

The Principles of Design

Dr. Ross[1] has shown that the various manifestations of order in design may be classified under three main general headings. In his different books there has been considerable variation in the terminology which he has used to indicate these categories or principles of order,

[1] *Op. cit.*

and other writers have used a great variety of terms usually without much attempt to classify them in a definite way. In this book I shall designate these principles of order as *harmony, sequence,* and *balance.*

By *harmony* is meant uniformity of any sort in the different parts of a composition, using the latter term in a very general sense; especially uniformity in which there is no definite feeling of change or movement, or definite feeling of opposition.

By *sequence* is meant uniformity in change or movement, producing a definitely felt progression; especially where there is uniformity or uniform change in the steps or differences between the separate parts of a series. The movement or change may be gradual or alternating. In the latter case it may be called rhythm.

By *balance* is meant uniformity in opposition of any sort.

All design may be regarded as an application of these principles to an arrangement of the terms of a particular art. It has been shown that, in drawing and painting, the terms are partly spatial — position, measure, and shape — and partly tonal — value, color, and intensity. It is not necessary, at the present moment, to elab-

69

orate these definitions in regard to their application to space relations, or to consider why only under proper circumstances does the apprehension of order result in aesthetic experience. The possible application of these different kinds of order to tone relations may be outlined briefly as follows.

HARMONY OF VALUES, COLORS, AND INTENSITIES

We may in the first place have harmony of value where all the tones of a composition are of exactly the same value, though perhaps varying in color and intensity. If all the tones are on the whole light, within the limits from HLt to LLt, for example; or on the whole dark, within the limits perhaps from HD to LD; or on the whole middling, within the limits perhaps from LLt to HD; there will be relative or approximate harmony as opposed to the lack of it in a range of values from Wt to Blk. This may be illustrated by holding pieces of paper over portions of the tones in Plate V and leaving only two or three adjacent horizontal rows visible. There is obviously an approximation to uniformity of value in the tones left visible, as compared with the variety of value in the whole chart. This relative

70

harmony of value is as a rule of greater importance in design than absolute uniformity of
value. It will be found an important element in
the design of many of the finest specimens of
Persian textiles, for example.

We may have absolute harmony of color
where all the tones of a composition are of exactly the same color, although varying possibly
in value and intensity; or we may have relative
harmony of color if the tones of a composition
are on the whole reddish, or on the whole yellowish, or on the whole bluish, or come within
any relatively limited range of color as compared with the variety of color in the whole
circle. This may be illustrated in Plate V by
covering over all but a few of the vertical rows
of the chart.

Harmony of intensity may also be absolute, if
all the tones in a composition are exactly the
same distance from neutral; or it may be relative, if all the tones in a composition are relatively low in intensity, or relatively high in intensity as compared with the complete range.
This is illustrated along the vertical rows in
Plate III.

Under ordinary circumstances a great variety
of values, colors, and intensities will seem cha-

otic and disorderly; on the other hand, great uniformity may seem monotonous and hence valueless artistically. Good designers, therefore, are constantly relieving uniformity of one factor by relative variety in one or both of the other factors; or, the other way round, introducing a harmony of one factor to compensate for variety in the others. Thus in much Persian painting it will be found that tones that are strongly contrasted in color are of the same or nearly the same value, especially if they are juxtaposed, while the strong value contrasts present little contrast of color and intensity. In a similar way in the Italian painting of the fourteenth and fifteenth centuries, where rather large fields of fairly intense color are often used for decorative surface effect, there is little emphasis on contrasts of light and dark, whereas Leonardo's extreme emphasis on contrasts of light and dark is accompanied by a wise suppression of color and intensity contrasts. Caravaggio, and Ribera, and Rembrandt also suppress color and intensity contrasts as they emphasize contrasts of light and shade. On the other hand, some of the worst tone design produced in the whole range of European painting, outside of the xix century, is found in the works of some of the xvi century painters who tried to combine the older decorative color with the light and shade of Leonardo.

Above we have outlined the possibilities of harmony in each of the three main factors of tone taken singly. We may of course have absolute or approximate harmony of all three factors together, or of any two factors without regard to the third factor. In the latter case we may use diagrams to illustrate some of the principal possibilities.

In the case of absolute harmony of value, color, and intensity, the result is monotony, which may, in some cases, be important in a single field but is of no significance in a whole composition. But approximate harmony of value, color, and intensity, where all the tones come within a relatively small part of the whole tone solid, may be of considerable significance. Approximate harmony of two factors, with a relatively wider range in the third factor, is still more important, and may be conveniently expressed in two-dimensional diagrams. Thus, given the tones, R, OY, Wt, G, BV, and Blk, as indicated in fig. 33 A, they may be harmonized more or less definitely by pulling them all toward Blk a smaller or greater distance. A common element of relative blackness will be introduced into all of the tones marked ', and still more strongly into all of the tones marked ". The possibility of similar harmonization toward Wt is shown in fig. 33 B; toward neutral-middle in fig. 33 C.

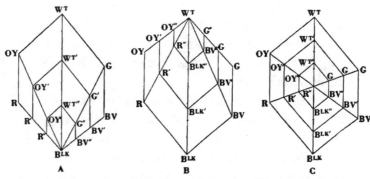

F<small>IG</small>. 33.   Harmonization by Reduction of Contrasts of Value and Intensity.

Exercises in which the tones are produced in a composition, first without harmonization, and then with harmonization in the different manners shown, will be found most helpful in illustrating the various possibilities of value and intensity harmony. Examples in nature will be found in the modelling of objects toward blackness in shadow, or their darkening as night comes on, their change toward Wt in reflected lights, or toward neutral gray in mist or fog.

Various possibilities of harmony of color and intensity are illustrated in figs. 34 and 35. Given the tones R, OY, G, and BV, as in fig. 34, they may be harmonized by pulling them all toward N in varying degrees, as in fig. 34 A, toward Y, as in fig. 34 B, or toward VR, as in fig. 34 C, without changing their relative contrasts with

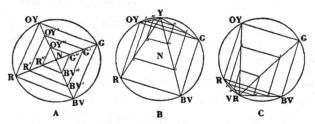

Fig. 34. Harmonization by Reduction of Contrasts of Color and Intensity.

each other. Exercises with actual tones are helpful to illustrate more clearly the possibilities of harmonization indicated in these diagrams also. Good examples in nature are to be found in harmonization under the influence of different colored lights, corresponding approximately to the changes indicated in the diagrams.

In most Venetian painting of the xvi century there is a distinctly golden tonality.[1] If what

[1] This is of course frequently exaggerated by the yellowing of oil and varnish in the course of time; but originally many of the paintings were probably decidedly golden in tone, made so, very

tells as white in a painting by Titian, for example, is compared with the Wt of white paper held in front of it, the white in the painting will be found to be in reality rather decided orange-yellow. It tells as Wt only in relation to the general tonality of the whole picture. By careful opposition of warm and cool tones, Titian makes his blues tell as very rich tones; but on being compared with intense blues, they are found to be as a matter of fact very low in intensity. The harmony of tonality in such a painting is perhaps best expressed in a diagram as in fig. 35A, or perhaps better in fig. 35 B. Although there is relative expression of practically all the colors in the color circle, there is actually used only a very limited range of colors and intensities, as compared with the whole color and intensity circle. It is common in such painting to make neutral, obtained by a mixture of white and black pigments, tell as relatively blue. In this case a mixture of red and neutral will tell as violet. Many paintings of the Renaissance, although expressing relatively warm and cool color, contain no positively cool tones at all. No green or blue pigments are employed in pro-

---

likely, to harmonize with heavy gilded mouldings used as enframements in the architectural decoration of the sixteenth century.

ducing them. Some of Rembrandt's portraits
are good examples.[1]

Other possibilities in the way of limited ranges
of colors and intensities are suggested in fig. 35 C
and D. The former approximates the harmony

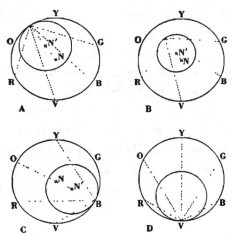

FIG. 35.   Use of Limited Ranges of Color and Intensity.

of bluish tonality found in some of Turner's
water-color paintings on blue-gray paper. Fig.
35 D indicates a possible violet tonality. There
are almost infinite possibilities in the way of
achieving harmony of tonality by the use of
such limited ranges of colors and intensities,

[1] This is discussed further in the next chapter in connection
with the abstract rendering of color relations.

without the sacrifice of relative variety of color. They can be applied to painting either in the mode of representation or in the mode of pure design.

A diagram like that shown in fig. 23 may be used, as explained on page 35, to indicate harmony of values and colors without regard to the question of intensities. The plotting of the tones of a fine textile, for example, will frequently reveal much of the secret of the tone harmony which it contains, by showing a surprisingly limited range of values. A limited range of color, from R to Y, for example, or from perhaps O to G, might also be exhibited clearly in this sort of diagram; but, as a rule, color must be considered along with intensity, and this diagram is not as useful as the others already described.

HARMONY OF ATTRACTION · QUANTITIES

In any composition the contrast of each tone with the adjacent tone or tones exerts a definite. attraction on the eye of greater or less power. If the attractions exerted by the tone contrasts in all the different parts of the composition are the same, there will be uniformity of attraction over the whole surface of the composition, resulting in a generally harmonious surface. This is an important consideration in all kinds of tone design. Fine and striking examples are to be found in Coptic textiles. Individual specimens vary in the strength of the attractions exerted by their design themes; but in any one the same force of attraction is maintained over the whole surface of the composition.

Another kind of harmony of attraction, which, so far as I know, has not been at all adequately discussed up to the present time, is obtained by achieving a uniformity of attraction of the tones employed in a composition, regardless of their distribution. The simplest possible illustration of this may be made by placing four or five different tones of equal area on a black ground-tone, allowing the black to show on all sides of each of the other tones. If the tones are, let us suppose, O–LLt, YG–Lt, GB–M, B–HD, and VR–D, the VR will make the least contrast with the Blk of the ground and will exert the least attraction of all the tones; the attraction of the B will be somewhat greater; that of the GB still greater; and that of the O and the YG greatest of all. There will be no uniformity of attraction, and practically no harmony of any kind in the tone arrangement. If, however, without changing in any way their values, colors, and intensities, the relative sizes of the different areas are changed, by cutting in with the Blk over the B, GB, YG, and O areas, the quantity of each of these other areas may be reduced until it exerts on the eye the same attraction as the larger quantity of the VR. Uniformity of attraction will then be achieved, and there will be a harmony in the whole arrangement entirely absent before. Curiously enough, this change in the quantity relations of the different areas will frequently almost make one believe that the quality of the individual tones has been changed.

As it takes some experience, even in this simple exercise, to achieve perfect uniformity of attraction, the working-out of problems in harmony of attraction is excellent as a means of training the eye in sensitiveness of reaction. The same exercise may be carried out on different ground tones. The relative quantities of the different tones will vary according to the contrasts made with the ground tone. If, for example, the tones cited above are placed on a Wt ground, the YG area will be largest, the O somewhat smaller, the GB and B still smaller, and the VR smallest of all. On an OY–Lt ground, the O and YG would be the larger areas, and the others would be much smaller, though just how much smaller must be determined by actual eye judgment.

This is the principle underlying the whole question of quantities — how much of each tone to use in a given composition. It seems to be a fundamental principle in much tone design. When there is a common ground-tone, the problem is comparatively simple. Good and striking examples are to be found in many Persian textiles, and in the stained-glass windows of the twelfth and, thirteenth centuries, in which the tones are all placed against the dark of the leads and the surrounding iron and stone enframement. The latter are also good examples of the other type of harmony of attraction referred to above.

When the tones are all juxtaposed, instead of isolated against a ground tone, and especially where limited tonalities are employed, the problem is much more complicated, but the end sought is the same. Values, colors, and intensities, together with quantities, may be so adjusted that the different tones attract the eye approximately with the same force. There is practically no difference in principle. As in the case of harmony of value, or color, or intensity, an approximation to uniform attraction will, in

81

some cases, serve to express the idea of harmony and satisfy the eye almost as well as absolute uniformity. It will depend more or less on the general nature of a composition just how exact the equality must be.

The possibility of a gradation of force in the attractions of the tones of simple patterns will be discussed under the heading of sequence.

HARMONY OF COLOR AND INTENSITY CONTRASTS

Another way of achieving a definite organization in tone relations might be spoken of as a harmony of color and intensity contrasts. If exactly the same intensities of different colors are used, placed against a neutral ground tone, there will be a definitely appreciable harmony in the equality of the contrasts between the background and each of the colored tones. This is indicated in fig. 36.

The same principle seems to apply if the ground tone is changed to a definite color, say OY of a low intensity, as in fig. 37. If on this ground tone are placed tones all at the same distance in color and intensity from the ground tone, there will be a definite uniformity of contrast in color and intensity between the different superposed tones and the ground tone; and this seems to be visually appreciable as a definite, but, off-hand, inexplicable harmony. I have never seen this particular possibility referred to in any book on design, but I have had students

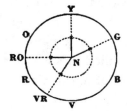

FIG. 36. Harmony of Color and Intensity Contrasts with Neutral Ground Tone

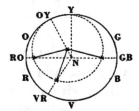

FIG. 37. Harmony of Color and Intensity Contrasts with Colored Ground Tone.[1]

experiment with the idea with very definite results. It first occurred to me in connection with a fragment of a Persian carpet in the Boston Museum, where there seemed to be just this definite uniformity of snap of color and intensity contrast between all the superposed tones

[1] To be perfectly accurate, this ought to be worked out on a circle with exact measures of color and intensity intervals.

83

and the ground. Some such principle is probably involved in compositions in which there is juxtaposition of the tones instead of a superposition on a uniform ground, but the problem becomes much more involved in this case. Further investigation along this general line, however, may enable us to discover a more definite principle that may be applied in such compositions than the mere matter of harmonization within a limited range of color and intensity.

What has been said above will at least suffice to outline some of the principal possibilities in connection with the application of the principle of harmony to tone relations, and to suggest avenues for further speculation and investigation. Unfortunately the subject cannot be discussed in great detail without recourse to illustration in actual color, and for this purpose the adjustment of tones has to be much more accurate than can be achieved in any ordinary method of color printing.

SEQUENCE

The subject of tone sequence may be dealt with in much more summary fashion than that of tone harmony, for it is on the whole more obvious, and examples will occur readily to everyone. Skies, birds' feathers, butterflies' wings, petals of flowers, and leaves of plants, are all familiar examples of regular gradation of value or color or intensity. Fields in design are also constantly organized by means of a gradation of tone. In borders of all kinds we find familiar examples of regular alternation of tones. It will hardly be necessary therefore to do more than for the sake of completeness list the possibilities with little comment.

We may have either gradual or alternate sequence of value, color, or intensity, or of any two, or of all three combined.

The tone contrasts and the tone quantities in a composition might be so arranged that there would be a regular gradation of the attractions of the different tones; but that this might make a definite appeal to the observer, the arrangement would have to be very simple. The importance of this form of sequence is, I believe, somewhat problematical, though theoretically it is a possibility. An alternation of attractions is, on the other hand, constantly found in rhythmical progressions.

As objects in nature model from light into shadow, the tones change in the form of a regular sequence, as indicated in fig. 20. The relations of the tones stay exactly the same in the different planes of modelling; but there is a proportional diminution of contrasts that produces a very definite organization in all the tones of a subject which is governed by a simple effect of lighting. The interest of interiors, like those painted by Vermeer and de Hoogh, depends largely on the presence of this definite sequence governing all the tone relations. Still-life subjects, as treated by Western painters, also owe a large part of their interest to the fact that the organization of the tones follows this principle. That is why many of the greatest masters from the seventeenth century down to our own day seem to have got more real fun out of the painting of these than of any other subjects. For the real connoisseur also, the "natures mortes," like those of Monet and Manet, little known by the general public, are perhaps the most nearly perfect performances of modern painting.

In painting, more or less arbitrary tone sequences established on the palette are of the greatest use in achieving definite organization in the tone relations. These may be used in such a way that the sequences are definitely felt in the resulting composition. OY-Lt, RO-M, and VR-D would be an example of a simple tone scheme in which there is a regular gradation of values and colors. Schemes of this sort, with varying intensities, may be used in pure design. Another simple example would be: Y–HLt, R–Lt, B–LLt, Y–M, R–HD, B–D. In this case there is a repetition of the value and color relations in two different value registers. YG–HLt, RO–Lt, BV–LLt, YG–M, RO–HD, BV–D would be another similar scheme.

This matter is discussed much more at length in the next chapter.

BALANCE

Balance in design consists, in its simplest form, in the achievement of an equilibrium in the attraction exerted by the various tone contrasts in a composition on either side of a vertical axis, or around a central point. In one case the balance may be called axial, in the other case, central. If the positions, measures, and shapes, and the tones are arranged in an exact opposition, either on the axis or on the center, as the case may be, the balance is obvious. If, on the other hand, the arrangement of tones does not correspond exactly to the arrangement of the positions, measures, and shapes, but there is at the same time an equality in the total tone attractions on either side of the axis or around the center, the balance may be called occult or irregular. Thus in a symmetrical arrangement of positions, measures, and shapes on either side of a vertical axis, as in some of the mediaeval or Renaissance paintings representing the Madonna and Saints, in which the measures and shapes of the fields on either side of the axis correspond almost exactly, a certain combination of tones on one side may be offset by an entirely different combination on the other, so long as the total attraction is the same. In many Persian carpets there is no exact correspondence of tones in the pattern on the two sides of the axis, but there is perfect balance of attractions. In a similar way, in asymmetrical arrangements of positions, measures, and shapes, a larger amount of a slight contrast on one side of an axis may produce the same attraction on the eye as that of a very strong contrast, but smaller in measure, on the other side. The general principle of the lever holds for balance of tones in this case: the farther the tone is from the axis or from the center, the stronger is its attraction.

The term balance may also properly be used in connection with another form of equal opposition or antithesis, where a composition is divided into equal areas of what are on the whole light tones, as compared with others which are on the whole dark. This type of balance is found in many of the later Renaissance landscape paintings. The composition must be fairly simple, and the lights and darks respectively well massed together, in order that the balance may be felt. Different colored fields might also be balanced in this way.

Inasmuch as the relations of colors are naturally expressed in a color circle, with approximate complementaries opposite, it has been supposed that there must be some virtue in a "balancing" of complementary pairs of colors, or in the adjustment of the tones of a composition in such a way that the average of all taken together should be neutral. In this case the balance would certainly have to be based on the true color circle obtained by the mixing of light, and not on the approximate color circle which applies to pigment mixtures. But I have never been able to feel that there was any virtue in attempted arrangements of this sort, or in the compositions cited as good examples of color balance, which could not be accounted for better on the hypothesis of harmony of attraction or harmony of tonality of some other sort. At any rate, there is no average of grayness in most of the Renaissance paintings; these almost all verge on a more or less golden tonality. Many fine Oriental and Western textiles also have distinct tonalities of various sorts other than neutral.

HARMONY, SEQUENCE, AND BALANCE IN CONNECTION WITH SATURATION AND BRIGHTNESS

The factors of saturation and brightness should be considered in connection with design; but, at present at least, I have little evidence to offer as to the practical significance of the principles of harmony, sequence, and balance as applied to these factors, as differentiated from a combination of value and intensity. Reference has been made above (p. 59) to harmony of brightness as a possible explanation of the consistency of quality in the tones used by painters like Monet and Renoir. I believe that harmony of saturation may be involved in the peculiar beauty of quality to be found in the tones of many textiles. So far as I know, little has been done in the way of experimentation on the basis of this idea.

Conclusion

These are some of the principal possibilities in the way of obtaining organization in tone relations. Each one, it must be remembered, is a possibility, not a requirement; and one cannot judge of the virtue of a composition simply by noting the presence or the absence of some one or two favorite theoretical possibilities. As has been shown above, there is almost a multitude of different ways of getting some sort of organization in the relation of tones in a composition. In order to achieve the kind of arrangement that may have aesthetic interest, there must be a manifestation of order; but there must usually be also a feeling of variety, of contrast, of disorder, within which the organization is accomplished, and which serves as a means to make the organization emotionally interesting. In certain cases where a uniform tone is required, as sometimes in the different fields of a composition, there may be a certain virtue in a complete uniformity of value, color, and intensity — at least a lack of it may disturb us; but in a whole composition such uniformity is mere monotony and uninteresting. So any approach to complete uniformity from many different points of view will tend to produce a monotonous and uninteresting effect. In the most interesting tone design the feeling of harmony produced is often quite unaccountable off-hand. There is a delightful sparkle of interest in unexpected juxtapositions and contrasts, and at the same time a pulling together of the separate elements by exact and just relationship of the value or color or intensity contrasts, or of the quantities of the different tones, to make a final grand organization of the whole design.

CHAPTER IV

TONE RELATIONS IN PAINTING

VALUE RELATIONS

IT IS well understood that the range of values in a painting seen in the diffused light of an ordinary room or gallery is very small, compared with the range of values in a sunlit landscape, or even in an interior where the light from a window shines directly upon the objects in a room and is reflected in their surfaces; and that in a painting only the relations of light and dark, and not the actual contrasts, can be expressed. But certain arbitrary distortions of the value relations which may be employed, and have actually been employed in certain types of painting of the past, are not so well understood.[1] Moreover, the possible variation in intensity range in painting as compared with that in nature, which is considered in the following section, has never been adequately discussed.

Normal Rendering of Value Relations

The diagram given in fig. 38 will do well enough to show the possible difference between

---

[1] Ruskin is the only writer, I believe, who has ever considered this problem at all. See *Modern Painters*, vol. IV, Part V, chap. 4, "Of Turnerian Light."

the range of values in nature and that in painting. The light of white in paint is far removed from that of white in nature. With the narrow range of values in painting it is impossible to express the strength of contrast between different parts of the value range in nature; and it is im-

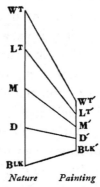

Nature   Painting

FIG. 38. Normal Rendering of Value Relations.

possible, if the main relations are preserved, to express anything like all of the details of form which in nature are clearly brought out by the wider contrasts. On the other hand, it is possible in painting to express the main relations of light and dark with perfect accuracy, as may be seen in fig. 38, where the distances from Blk to D to M to Lt to Wt in painting are proportional to those in nature, though to attain this accurate rendering of nature great judgment is required on the

94

part of the painter, who must be something more than a mere matcher of tones. Perhaps the best examples of what we may call this "normal method" of rendering value relations are to be found in the best works of Vermeer, in "Las Meniñas" and the "Villa Medici" by Velazquez, in some of Corot's earlier works, and in some of the paintings of Turner's middle period.

Crowding of the Darks

Let us suppose that for some reason or other the painter is not so much interested in an accurate rendering of the proportional value relations, but is especially interested in the strength of the contrasts in the lighter tones, and in the strong contrast between these and the principal darker tones. Instead of maintaining the distances of Blk to D to M to Lt to Wt in their true relation, he may extend the upper part of the value scale, and crowd the lower part, as in fig. 39. The painting will then be a distortion of the proportional relations; but it may possibly express his ideas better, or it may give him a general tonality, or make possible a type of composition which is more suitable to his particular requirements. In this case the distortion is perfectly justifiable. In all cases, of course, it is

95

finally a question of aesthetic result. Examples of compositions based on "crowding of the darks" in this fashion are to be found in the works of Caravaggio, Ribera, Rembrandt, Hobbema, Ruysdael, and other Dutch landscape painters, and of Poussin, Claude, Wilson, and

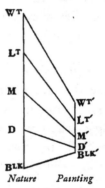

Nature   Painting

Fig. 39. Crowding of the Darks.

Turner. In many cases, this scheme is used in connection with the rendering of an effect of concentrated light which in nature would actually produce something of the same result; but it is notable that in many other paintings the same arrangement of values is maintained. Almost all xvii and xviii century landscape paintings show very dark masses in the foreground to set off the lighter tones of the middle distance and distance, where the main interest

96

is concentrated; and the composition regularly proceeds from dark foreground through a series of two or three lighter planes to the distance. Even in sea-pieces, like those of Van de Velde, the immediate "foreground" is regularly darkened. In landscapes the effect is often as if a huge canopy were suspended over the foreground, from under which the observer looks off into the sunlit distance. The "View of Delft" by Vermeer, in the museum at the Hague, is one of the few landscapes of the XVII century in which the foreground is not arbitrarily darkened and the values are rendered throughout in their normal relations.

In figure painting "crowding of the darks" usually produces a sensational effect of large masses of extreme dark, relieved by small spots of gleaming light. This effect was definitely sought for by many of the later-Renaissance painters, beginning with Leonardo da Vinci. It goes along with the general sensationalism of much of this painting. In the Baroque epoch of the later XVI and XVII centuries, Caravaggio was the principal innovator in the use of concentrated light effect. Guido Reni, Guercino, and almost all of the Italian painters of the XVII century borrowed the scheme; it was also imitated by many of the northern painters who studied in Italy, as shown in some of the early works of Rubens and Van Dyck; and the Spanish-Neapolitan painter, Ribera, made it a principal means for the expression of his sensational conceptions.

Crowding of the Lights

Turner, in some of his later work, and other painters, like Monet for instance, following his

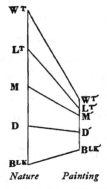

Nature   Painting

Fig. 40. Crowding of the Lights.

example, have tried to achieve more and more of an impression of illumination in the composition as a whole by exactly reversing this process and crowding the lights, instead of the darks, as shown in fig. 40. In this case, the canvas tends on the whole to become a glare of light, with very slight contrasts and little indication of detail in the lighter portions, and with perhaps a few small accents of darker tones in the foreground. This has often been supposed to come closer to nature, but it is in reality just as arbitrary as the crowding of the darks.

Crowding of both Lights and Darks

Rembrandt, in some of his works, crowds both ends of the value range, as shown in fig. 41, slid-

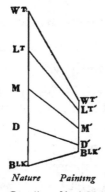

Nature   Painting

FIG. 41. Crowding of both Lights and Darks.

ing over the intermediate tones rapidly, and thereby increasing the effect of the contrast between light and dark. In the work of many figure and portrait painters a slight pulling-up of the darks and half-lights in the planes turned toward the light is used to increase the effect of broad illumination in such passages. Examples are to be found in the portraits of Reynolds and of other English painters.

I do not mean to suggest that painters have worked directly from nature, consciously distorting value relations in this way; but the various hypotheses indicated in these diagrams will serve to explain the general conceptions which, on different occasions, governed the painters' interpretations of the effect of light and dark.

INTENSITY RELATIONS

Normal Intensity Range

In a similar way it will be seen from fig. 42 that the possible intensity range in nature is much greater than that in painting, but that the relations of intensities to values in nature may be accurately expressed in their true proportion in painting. To represent the possibilities as clearly as possible, let us suppose that we have one tone in nature, a in fig. 43 A. Within the narrower limits of values and intensities in painting, b in fig. 43 B represents its intensity in relation to the value range in true proportion. This, shown also in fig. 43 B', we may call the "normal rendering of intensity relations." The "View of Delft" by Vermeer, many paintings by Corot, many by Constable, many by Turner from his middle period, a painting like the "Westminster Bridge," by Whistler, as well as many early works by Monet and Pissaro, may be cited as examples of this normal method of painting.

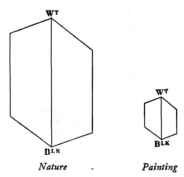

Nature *Painting*

FIG. 42. Limitation of Intensity Range Corresponding to Limitation of Value Range.

Suppressed Intensity Range

On the other hand, many painters, particularly landscape painters of the XVII and XVIII centuries, perhaps partly on account of custom, or because of limitations of pigment materials, or for the sake of greater tone harmony, have arbitrarily expressed themselves in what we may call a "suppressed" intensity range. In this case *a* of fig. 43 A is represented by *c* in C. This, shown also in fig. 43 C', produces an effect of very subdued color. Relative degrees of intensity are of course represented within this narrower

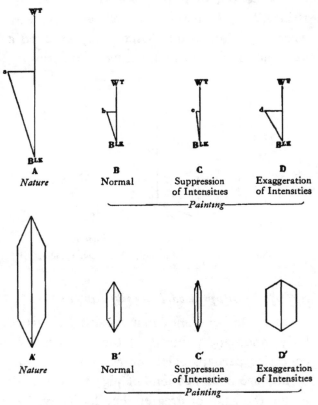

FIG. 43. Varying Ranges of Intensity in Painting.

range. In addition to painters of the XVII and XVIII centuries, who for the most part used warm golden tonalities, Whistler in the XIX century very frequently suppressed the range of intensities in a perfectly arbitrary fashion for the sake of greater tone harmony.

Exaggerated Intensity Range

Still other painters in recent times have attempted to express more of the positive intensity of color in nature and more of the total brilliance of out-of-door contrasts by exaggerating the intensity range in relation to the value range. In this case *a* of fig. 43 A is rendered perhaps by *d* in D. The same idea is shown also in fig. 41 D'. By means somewhat on this order, painters like Monet, Renoir, Dodge MacKnight, and perhaps Turner in some of his later work, though he was more often merely handling especially brilliant effects in nature in a nearly normal manner, have been able in a measure to compensate for the loss of value contrasts in painting, by substituting greater proportional color and intensity contrasts, and in this arbitrary manner to express something of the emotional reaction which they have felt in the presence of nature. As a matter of fact most of these painters have tended to transpose the tones of nature into a harmony of highest possible brightness, as has been suggested on page 59. They have laid out on their palettes only pigments of high intensity from red around to violet, and have mixed these only with adjacent colors or with white. This is, I believe, the real explanation of the special qualities of the palette employed by Monet, instead of the pseudo-scientific theory of the breaking-up of light into all the colors of the spectrum usually offered. The transposition from nature is perfectly arbitrary. When the average untrained observer objects to the tones in these paintings as untruthful, he is usually told that this is the way the painter sees them in nature. It is nothing of the sort. The painter makes an arbitrary transposition into a scheme of his own for the sake of expressing what he considers most important in the organization of the tones in nature, and to express more convincingly his emotional reaction. Everyone has in a way to get used to the conventions employed before he can understand what the painter is driving at. It is seldom anyone is able to understand a picture by Dodge MacKnight, for instance, the first time that he sees any of this painter's work; there are few who do not take these paintings as a matter of course in a short time.

Color Relations

At the present day there is a rather generally accepted popular notion that an artist, when he paints from nature, should try to copy down the tones in his subject exactly as he sees them, rendering not only the variations of value and intensity but also all their exact variations of color. This is what students are ordinarily taught to do, as far as is possible, in the art schools. That is what most people, I suppose, understand by the phrase "learning to paint." Moreover, the modern naturalist painter, whether "pointillistic," like Monet, or broadly impressionistic, like Sargent, has thought of his painting as an imitation of the cross-section of the rays of light travelling toward the eye, in a plane at a distance corresponding to the normal distance of the picture from the eye. The so-called impressionists emphasized the main relations of the different parts of this cross-section in "broken color" technique, and ignored precise details of form and of local tone; other painters may have sought to distinguish individual objects in form and texture more completely. In any case, the object of all these painters has been to render the main variations of tone in an imitative fashion. As a matter of fact, even in the xix century and at the present day, the most naturalistic painters have actually practised within conventions much more limited than is popularly supposed, or than they themselves have imagined in many cases. Almost every painter has, in the course of time, adopted at least a more or less limited range of pigments, and has got into the habit of adapting his expression, and even his vision, to the possibilities of his particular palette. In the case of painters before the xix century the idea of rendering the color of nature in an imitative fashion probably never occurred to anyone. Painters constantly interpreted nature in a vocabulary of tone which was always based on that prescribed by the master in the workshop, and was then possibly varied somewhat according to the individual painter's particular purpose. The rendering of color was always a matter of the *expression* of what seemed essential relations within conventional limitations, and not at all a matter of an *imitation* of all the variations of color in the subject itself.

In a drawing which shows merely the relative illumination of surface in light and shade, it is possible to express the main effect of light and shadow by an arbitrary abstraction into two values — perhaps white paper for all the lighter tones, and a wash of bistre or sepia or gray for all the tones that are on the whole dark, although there may be a considerable range of values in both lights and darks in the subject itself. Some of Tiepolo's wash drawings illustrate this method of abstract expression which will be discussed more at length in connection with the different modes of drawing in the second volume. We should be making use of much the same sort of abstraction if, in a painting, we were to express all the different warm colors in a subject by some one warm color, perhaps orange, and all the cool colors by some one cool color, perhaps blue or green-blue, as shown in the diagram in fig. 44 A. We may draw a dividing line anywhere we like — letting O stand for all colors on one side of the line, and B for all the colors on the other side. In this case the line suggested is through YG–N–VR. If we use orange and blue pigments, with white and black, to obtain different values, we may mix the orange and the blue together to get different intensities of each color, or possibly neutral — any tone, that is, along the line O–N–B. By varying intensities of the orange and blue along this line, we may actually indicate a good deal of the essential effect of color in a composition; by inference — that is, by association in this case — we may even suggest some actual variation of color beyond the two employed. Essentially, however, it is an abstract rendering of merely the main relations of warm

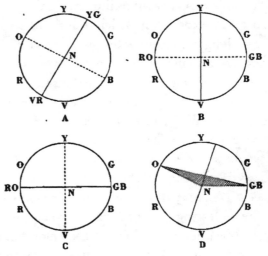

FIG. 44. Varying Ranges of Color.

and cool tones, without regard to exact variations of hue or specific color. For many purposes this may be all that we want—in fact, on account of the ease of expression or the harmony of tone involved, it may be preferable in many cases to an attempt to render all the variations of color that exist in the subject itself.

One may make an arbitrary rendering of color in this way with any pair of complementary colors, according to the particular tonality in the subject which it may be desirable to emphasize, as in fig. 44 B and C; or one may use approximate complementaries as is indicated in fig. 44 D. In this case the mixture of the two colors will give low intensities of the intermediate colors on one side of neutral; but the abstraction is nearly as complete as with exact complementaries.

Common examples of such abstract renderings of main color relations, as, for example, red and neutral, are to be found in the reproductions on certain magazine or periodical covers. Some of the colored "movies" are also based on an abstraction into a warm color like red-orange and a cool color like green-blue. These might or might not be exact complementaries in subtractive mixing; they would probably give a slightly more naturalistic effect, if they were not exact complementaries.

In the painting of the Renaissance this kind of abstract rendering of color is often found. Good examples are the landscape backgrounds in some of the Florentine and Umbro-Florentine paintings of the xv century, as in those by Antonio Pollaiuolo and Piero dei Franceschi. In

109

these it is a mere matter of a play of color obtained by the use of brownish and bluish pigments — usually a low intensity orange or orange-yellow, and a green-blue. In the distances of some of the landscapes by Claude Lorrain and Poussin in the xvii century it also seems to come down frequently to an abstraction into a relative warm and a relative cool obtained by brown and blue pigments.

It is frequently pointed out by psychologists that a small field of neutral gray placed in the middle of a field of color will, by inference, appear to be the complementary color in a low intensity. So if we place a neutral in the midst of a field of red, or red-orange, the neutral will tell as a positively cool color, GB or B. Therefore the color in a subject might be rendered abstractly by a mere play of a warm color and the relative cool color of neutral.

From the xvi century right down through the later Renaissance the variations of warm and cool color in flesh tone and even in a whole subject are constantly rendered in precisely this way, in a play of neutral (white and black) with a red or a red-orange, or, as in some Baroque paintings, even orange or orange-yellow, sometimes probably with final glazes of yellow or with some accents of yellow. The "Athenaeum Portrait of Washington," by Gilbert Stuart, in the Boston Museum, is a good illustration of the possibilities of such abstraction. The eyes, for example, tell as decided blue; but this is achieved only with a mixture of white and black pigment, relieved against the ruddy tone of the flesh.

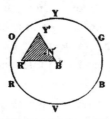

Fig. 45. Limited Range of Color and Intensity in much Renaissance Painting.

If one were to add a yellow pigment to the palette of red and neutral just suggested, one would still have a decidedly limited and abstract palette, as shown in fig. 45; but it would lend itself to a suggestion of considerably more variety of color. In this case there would be a distinct harmonization of color within the approximate smaller circle. The mixtures of pigments — perhaps Venetian red, yellow ochre and white and black — would achieve actual colors within the triangle R'–Y'–B', which is a

III

decided positive harmony of color and intensity in the painting surface as a whole, if one has regard for its significance as decoration in a room; but, as in this general tonality the positive neutral would tell as a low intensity blue, relative neutral in the painting would be represented by a positive orange or orange-yellow. Therefore within the positive harmony of color we might have an expression or indication of a considerable variety of color — thus orange between R' and Y', green between Y' and B', and even a definite suggestion of violet between_R' and B', B' in this case being actually a neutral obtained by a mixture of white and black pigments. In the Ross Collection at the Boston Museum[1] there are two small paintings of landscapes with figures, probably by some Italian painter of about 1700, in which there is an effect of great variety as well as richness of color. In these paintings there are tones which tell as decided blues and greens and violets, along with the warmer tones of reds and browns and yellows, and one would off-hand suppose that a blue pigment must have been used in painting them; but, by actual experiment, it has been

[1] These are, at the time of writing, on indefinite loan at the Fogg Museum.

found that the tones which tell as decided blues are nothing but a mixture of white and black, and that this actual neutral is mixed with yellow and red to produce the relative greens and violets. This limited palette, which conditioned an abstract rendering of color relations, was used constantly during the later Renaissance, from the xvi to the end of the xviii century, and in many paintings also of the xix century, especially in those, like some of Manet's, which derived from an adaptation of earlier Renaissance tonalities. This palette meant a very decided harmony of color and intensity in the painting as a whole, and the resulting tonality usually fitted in very well with the general decorative schemes of the rooms in the houses and palaces of the later Renaissance. More extended ranges were also used, with positive greens and blues; usually, however, these were not very intense, and violets and blue-violets were ordinarily left out entirely, so that the range of colors and intensities was always fairly limited. Pictorial color was based for the most part on a harmony of orange or orange-yellow tonality.

Practically none of the painting of the Renaissance, even at its most naturalistic, was a matching of colors in the manner assumed popularly at the present day. It was always a transposition into a more or less restricted vocabulary, often highly abstract. Naturally, the vocabulary of color is found to be much more conventional if one goes back to the completely non-naturalistic painting done before the xvi century.

What has been said above suggests something of the kind of abstract rendering of color com-

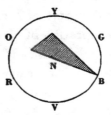

Fɪɢ. 46. Limited Range of Color and Intensity used in Certain Types of Landscape Painting.

mon to painting in the later Renaissance. Many variations are of course possible. In much landscape painting of the xvii, xviii, and early xix centuries, as in the early Turners and in many Corots, one finds a limited color range something like that indicated in fig. 46, which would depend on the use of a brown pigment, like burnt sienna, a yellow like yellow ochre, and a blue like Prussian or cobalt blue. A Venetian red, instead of burnt sienna, might be

114

used to extend the palette down to red-orange; or Venetian red and Indian red, or even vermilion, might be used for occasional small accents, as in the figures, without altering the general scheme.

A combination of red, yellow, and blue pigments is frequently used in painting. Even

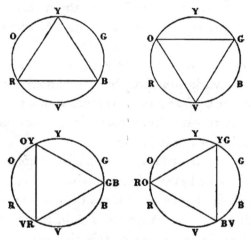

FIG. 47. Limitation of Color and Intensity in Principal Triads.

with high intensities, this means more limitation of color and intensity than is often supposed, for the orange, green, and violet intermediates cannot be achieved in quite the intensities of the main red, yellow, and blue tones. With low intensities of the main tones, the limitations are naturally greater throughout.

115

Other "triads" of color might also be used, as indicated in fig. 47, which shows the most obvious ones to be derived from the scale of twelve colors. Each of these presents a special case of limitation of intensity, according to what are taken as main colors and what as intermediates. Sets of three colors taken at unequal, instead of equal, intervals in the twelve-color scale might also be used, as in fig. 46, which has already been referred to. Also the intensities may be varied. Using only three colors in this way, the variations possible are almost endless; but the use of any one involves a more or less arbitrary transposition from the tones of nature into those of the painting.

As a matter of fact, a naturalistic effect may be maintained even when the abstraction is carried still farther in some ways than it was in the painting of the Renaissance. For instance, it was stated at the beginning of this chapter that one might abstract all the warm and cool tones in a subject into two colors, one warm and one cool, and still obtain in many cases a good deal of natural effect. Suppose that in making a painting in this way we were to use a red-orange for the warm tones and a green-blue for the cool tones. If we were to paint in oils, we could make our painting very conveniently by arranging our palette, very much after the manner of later Renaissance painters, in a series of different values of red-orange on one side, and different values of green-blue on the other, thus:

	Wt	
RO	(Hlt)	GB
RO	(Lt)	GB
RO	(Llt)	GB
RO	(M)	GB
RO	(Hd)	GB
RO	(D)	GB
RO	(Ld)	GB
	Blk	

Fig. 48. Palette of Complementary Pairs.

With this arrangement we can easily get any value and any intensity of the warm or cool color that we require by mixing the tones straight across, controlling the intensity of the RO by its complementary GB, or the other way round, neutralizing the GB as required by mixing in RO at the same value, or by mixing adjacent tones up and down for intermediate values. In fig. 48 we have indicated a palette of seven registers, or value levels, between white and black. With an arrangement of this sort we shall be able to suggest a good deal of complete color effect; but we may find the result too monotonous for some purposes, in that exactly the same color combinations are repeated at all the different values between white and black.

To avoid this monotony, suppose that instead of using red-orange and green-blue all the way up and down, we change the color slightly from register to register, but still keep a complementary pair of colors, and so an abstraction into two colors, to represent opposite sides of the color circle in each value level or register. We should then have a palette like one of the following:

Wt			Wt	
Y	V		V	Y
OY	BV		VR	YG
O	B		R	G
RO	GB		RO	GB
R	G		O	B
VR	YG		OY	BV
V	Y		Y	V
Blk			Blk	

Fig. 49. Palettes with Different Complementary Pairs in Successive Values.

In each of these examples we have the possibility of expressing the relative color and intensity by the mixing of complementary pairs at the different value levels; but there is a gradual sequence of color up and down the value registers — a perfectly ordered arrangement, but one that gives greater variety than the repetitions of the same colors in fig. 48.

This is carrying the idea of abstract expression of color and intensity relations somewhat farther than it was carried in the Renaissance; but the general idea involved is precisely the same. A completely naturalistic effect may be obtained within the limits of these abstract palettes, which offer the advantages of a simplified vocabulary of tone, and at the same time ensure some definite ordering of the tones from the standpoint of design.

What has been written above suggests the fundamental principles involved in the use of limited vocabularies of tone in all types of painting. In practically all painting there is more or less abstraction in the expression of color relations. The arrangements of tones on the palette shown in figs. 48 and 49 may be thought of as scaled palettes, or tone sequences. The use of these may more conveniently be discussed in a separate chapter.

CHAPTER V

SCALED PALETTES

INTRODUCTORY

As suggested in the last chapter, there is nothing particularly new in the use of limited ranges of color in painting, or in the laying-out of the palette in a precise and orderly fashion to facilitate the actual work of preparing the proper tones and putting them on the canvas, or panel, or wall. This was a common procedure throughout the Renaissance and down to the end of the XVIII century. During all this time the artist was always trained in the actual practice of painting in the workshop of the master; and from his master he acquired a vocabulary of tone by which to express himself, just as early Renaissance artists acquired a definite vocabulary of line largely by copying the drawings of the master.

In the XIX century, for a variety of causes, the artist came to be trained in a different way. The art school largely took the place of the workshop, and the idea of complete imitation of natural effect took the place of the idea of expression of essential relations within abstract limits, subordinated more or less to exigencies of design. Something of the older idea seems to have survived to some extent in certain of the studios of the xix century; and toward the end of the century a few painters attempted to get back something of what might be called the "expressional" methods and ideas of the Renaissance. Whistler probably went farther with this than almost any other painter in experimenting with definite arrangements of tone which he laid out on his palette and used in an abstract rendering of color and intensity relations. But Whistler had no follower who understood what he was driving at, and so he remains one of the isolated experimenters of the xix century. No doubt painters like Monet and Renoir had in mind a more complete naturalism, rather than arbitrary limitation in the manner of Whistler; nevertheless their palettes were decidedly abstract, for the tones they employed in their typical work of the 'eighties were limited approximately to the upper surface of the tone solid — that is, tones at full intensity, or between full intensity and white, with juxtaposition of these at about the same value level.

In the painting of the Renaissance and even in that of the later xix century, as in the case of Whistler and of Monet and Renoir, the use of limited ranges of color was largely empirical; it was merely a matter of workshop tradition or of individual experiment with pigment materials, with little theoretical basis. About twenty-five or thirty years ago Dr. Denman Ross — I have always suspected he got his first inspiration from Whistler's practice — began a series of experiments in the use of definitely arranged palettes based on a theoretical classification of tone relations. These experiments have been published in a succession of books, which, considered historically, take their place as part of the general modernistic reaction against the over-imitative aims of much XIX century painting.[1] It is not my present purpose to go into an elaborate discussion of these books or of the various experiments that have been made by Dr. Ross and others in connection with the use of different palettes; but I wish to propose a simple classification of all possible tone scales into a few main types, which will, I think, make the fundamental principles involved in the use of all scaled palettes — both those based on theoretical classifi-

[1] *A Theory of Pure Design, On Drawing and Painting,* and *The Painter's Palette,* to which reference has already been made.

cation of tones and those based on workshop tradition — more easily understood.

All definitely arranged palettes that can be used in representational painting owe their virtue to a regular repetition of certain color relations at different value levels between white and black. The different tones of the palette are mixed up separately and placed on the palette in a regular order, making a definite set of tones within the limits of which the painting may be produced. The range of colors and of intensities, as well as the width of the steps from value to value and from color to color, may be varied practically to infinity, but on the whole the scales fall into two main types, which we may call Type A and Type B respectively.

Type A

What may for convenience be called Type A scales include those in which there is a repetition of the same colors in a regular succession of values, known as value registers. The same colors occur in the same relation in each value register.

Triads

In what we may call triad scales, there are three colors in each value register. Ordinarily it will be found most convenient to choose these colors at approximately equal intervals in the color circle; but any set of three may be used, as illustrated in fig. 50. The colors and the approxi-

	Wᴛ				Wᴛ				Wᴛ		
HLᴛ	R	Y	B		O	G	V		VR	OY	GB
Lᴛ	R	Y	B		O	G	V		VR	OY	GB
LLᴛ	R	Y	B		O	G	V		VR	OY	GB
M	R	Y	B		O	G	V		VR	OY	GB
HD	R	Y	B		O	G	V		VR	OY	GB
D	R	Y	B		O	G	V		VR	OY	GB
LD	R	Y	B		O	G	V		VR	OY	GB
	Bʟᴋ				Bʟᴋ				Bʟᴋ		

A   B   C

Wᴛ			Wᴛ			Wᴛ		
RO	YG	BV	O	Y	B	R	Y	N
RO	YG	BV	O	Y	B	R	Y	N
RO	YG	BV	O	Y	B	R	Y	N
RO	YG	BV	O	Y	B	R	Y	N
RO	YG	BV	O	Y	B	R	Y	N
RO	YG	BV	O	Y	B	R	Y	N
RO	YG	BV	O	Y	B	R	Y	N
Bʟᴋ			Bʟᴋ			Bʟᴋ		

D   E   F

Fɪɢ. 50. Type A Palettes — Triads.

mate intensities, which can be obtained by mixing in each register, are shown in the circular diagrams below the different scales. The intensity of the original tones of the scale may be varied indefinitely, according to the pigments employed. In fig. 50 E is represented the scale which would be made by limiting the pigments employed to burnt sienna, yellow ochre, cobalt blue, and white. This is about the range of color and intensity to be found in much landscape painting of the xvii, xviii, and early xix centuries.

Complementary Pairs

Instead of three colors in each register, two colors which are complementary, or nearly so, may be used (fig. 51). This makes possible only a very limited range of color and intensity; but, as was pointed out in the last chapter, it is surprising how much naturalism of effect can be produced by the expression merely of different intensities in tones relatively warm and relatively cool. It is an abstract method of representation, in which all the possible colors are generalized into two opposing colors on either side of the color circle. G and H in fig. 51 illustrate approximately color ranges to be found in some of the landscape backgrounds of early-Renaissance paintings, and in some landscape paintings of the xvii century. In fig. 51 I, the range of color is similar to that found in much of the painting of flesh in fresco and tempera in the Renaissance; the same scheme was probably used in the underpainting for flesh in some types

Wt		Wt		Wt		Wt		Wt	
Y	V	OY	BV	O	B	RO	GB	R	G
Y	V	OY	BV	O	B	RO	GB	R	G
Y	V	OY	BV	O	B	RO	GB	R	G
Y	V	OY	BV	O	B	RO	GB	R	G
Y	V	OY	BV	O	B	RO	GB	R	G
Y	V	OY	BV	O	B	RO	GB	R	G
Y	V	OY	BV	O	B	RO	GB	R	G
Blk		Blk		Blk		Blk		Blk	

A   B   C   D   E

Wt		Wt		Wt		Wt		Wt	
VR	YG	O	GB	OY	B	RO	G	R	N
VR	YG	O	GB	OY	B	RO	G	R	N
VR	YG	O	GB	OY	B	RO	G	R	N
VR	YG	O	GB	OY	B	RO	G	R	N
VR	YG	O	GB	OY	B	RO	G	R	N
VR	YG	O	GB	OY	B	RO	G	R	N
VR	YG	O	GB	OY	B	RO	G	R	N
Blk		Blk		Blk		Blk		Blk	

F   G   H   I   J

Fig. 51.   Type A Palettes—Complementary Pairs.

of painting in the later Renaissance. Fig. 51 J represents a scale limited in color to R and N, as in the underpainting used for flesh and to some extent for other fields in much Venetian painting of the xvi century. A final glaze of yellow over a preparation of R and N would turn the whole painting into a triad scheme based on R, Y, and N, similar to the arrangement shown in fig. 50 F.[1]

Four or even five or more colors might be used in Type A scales. A scale like that in fig. 52 is an interesting possibility. The palettes used in the XVII and XVIII centuries would probably

	Wt		
R	Y	G	B
R	Y	G	B
R	Y	G	B
R	Y	G	B
R	Y	G	B
R	Y	G	B
R	Y	G	B
	Blk		

Fig. 52. Type A Palette with Four Colors.

show several columns of color arranged in this manner, if they were plotted out in diagrammatic form.

In all the scales indicated above, as well as in those of Type B which follow, variations in the intensity of a given color depend on a mixing with the complementary color in the same or the

[1] The neutral tones need not necessarily be obtained by a mixture of white and black pigments; a low orange pigment, like burnt sienna, mixed with French ultramarine, gives an approximate black which is for some purposes more satisfactory than any black pigment.

127

adjacent registers. For certain types of painting, a scale might be made in which the relative intensities of the main planes of light, half-light, and shadow, for the modelling of each object, would be fixed on the palette. In this case, there would be a separate column of tones for each field in the painting. For a yellow drapery, for

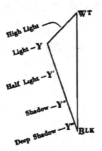

FIG. 53. Diagram for Tones of Single Color in a Palette Designed to Show Proportional Diminution of Intensities in Each Field.

example, as shown in fig. 53, the adjustment of values and intensities will follow the general scheme of the diagram in fig. 20. Any desired number of tones from the line Y–Blk may be set out on the palette — three or four would ordinarily be sufficient — for the modelling from the plane of light down to the deep shadows. Highlights will come from the line Y–Wt. The tone of each object in the plane of light is in this manner placed on the palette, and then the darker and

128

lighter tones required determined from this. A scheme somewhat like this was possibly used by Vermeer. In his painting the fields are quite distinct, and reflections are ignored to some extent; but the intensities in the different planes of light are very carefully adjusted to render clearly the proportional diminution of values and intensities as objects model down into shadow. In such painting the reflection of one object in the surface of another, or the reflection of light from the surface of one object on that of another may be rendered by a slight playing together of the scales of the separate objects.[1] In painting of this sort, there will be little of the harmony of tone referred to later on, which is due to the feeling of a single palette forming the basis for all the tones in the composition; moreover, there is a danger of getting an over-monotonous effect in the separate fields in place of the play or vibration of color that can be obtained in the case of the more usual palettes; but feeling of existence in space and atmosphere may be fairly easily achieved with this palette. Harmony will de-

[1] In *Modern Color*, by Cutler and Pepper (Harvard University Press, 1923), the use of a color top to ensure an accurate carrying down of the tones toward black and up to white is suggested. The frequent neutralization in the half-light as an object rounds into shadow, may also be worked out in this way.

pend on the exactness of the adjustment of value and intensity relations, and on the adjustment of the contrasts of the tones of the different fields.

TYPE B

What may be distinguished as Type B scales include those in which there is a regular sequence of color from register to register, with the relations of colors within the separate registers

Wt	
Y	V
OY	BV
O	B
RO	GB
R	G
VR	YG
V	Y
Blk	

Fig. 54. Type B Palette — Complementary Pairs with Warm Colors at Full Intensity.

remaining approximately uniform, as illustrated in fig. 54 and in others following.

Complementary Pairs

In fig. 51 D is shown a scale in which RO and GB are repeated in all the different registers. Let us suppose that RO and GB are kept in the M register, but that in the register next above

130

the complementary pair is changed to that of O
and B, the next above that to OY and BV, and
the next to Y and V. If the same movement is
continued downward below middle, the scale
shown in fig. 54 will be formed. This is the same
as in fig. 49 in the last chapter. In this the ex-

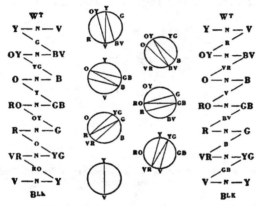

FIG. 55.   Type B Palette with Indication of Tones Derived
by Mixing Adjacents.

pression in each register is limited to the range
of a complementary pair, as in Type A scales;
but in the scale as a whole there is a much
greater variety of color, though limited to a
very definite sequence. Furthermore, still greater
variety of color may be obtained by mixing between registers on diagonals, as seen in fig. 55;
but the tones here fall also into very definite

131

sequences of color. In this scale, the colors Y, OY, O, RO, R, VR, V, all come at their normal value levels in the tone solid, and may be obtained at their highest intensities.

Another scale may be made in which also we keep RO and GB in the M register, but in which we proceed in the registers above to G and R,

	Wᴛ
V	Y
VR	YG
R	G
RO	GB
O	B
OY	BV
Y	V
	Bʟᴋ

Fɪɢ. 56.   Type B Palette — Complementary Pairs with Cool
Colors at Full Intensity.

then YG and VR, and Y and V, in order, and below, to B and O, BV and OY, and V and Y, as in fig. 56. In this scale, Y, YG, G, GB, B, BV, and V come at their normal value levels, and each one of these may be obtained at its highest intensity. The tones obtained by mixture in this scale are shown in fig. 57. In this, as in the preceding scale, a great variety of color may be obtained, but also all within definite sequences.

Either one of these scales may be used sepa-

132

rately, or they may be used together, as long as
they are not mixed across so as to destroy the
feeling of the sequences which are clearly indicated in all the vertical series in figs. 55 and 57.
The arrangement of the palette in this case is
shown in fig. 58.

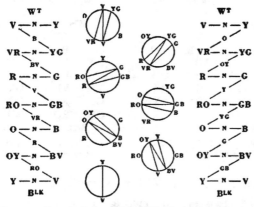

FIG. 57. Type B Palette with Indication of Tones Derived
by Mixing Adjacents.

This palette, with the possible variations in its
use, is discussed at length in Dr. Ross's *The
Painter's Palette.* The two scales, either together
or singly, have been used for several years in the
courses in painting in Harvard College; they are,
I believe, especially satisfactory for the beginner,
for, although they are very abstract and necessi-
tate definite thinking and clean handling, taken

133

together they command a range of color with which the local tone of practically any object can be indicated. For many purposes, other perhaps more limited palettes have advantages for the practised painter.

By varying the value levels of the complementary pairs, other similar scales may be

Wt		Wt	
Y	V	V	Y
OY	BV	VR	YG
O	B	R	G
RO	GB	RO	GB
R	G	O	B
VR	YG	OY	BV
V	Y	Y	V
Blk		Blk	

Fig. 58. Double Type B Palettes with RO and GB at M.

Wt		Wt	
RO	GB	GB	RO
O	B	G	R
OY	BV	YG	VR
Y	V	Y	V
YG	VR	OY	BV
G	R	O	B
GB	RO	RO	GB
Blk		Blk	

Fig. 59. Double Type B Palettes with Y and V at M.

formed. If Y and V, for example, are placed in the M register, the two scales shown in fig. 59 will be formed. Keeping to seven value registers between Wt and Blk, as in the simple value scale described in Chapter I, twelve different scales may be formed on this principle. With variations in the number of value registers and in the intervals between the colors, different scales of this type, all perfectly orderly and perfectly usable, may be formed practically to infinity.

Triads

Triad arrangements of colors may be used in Type B scales also. A few examples are given in fig. 60. These also may be varied practically endlessly. In general, however, scales of this sort are almost too cumbersome; they offer more tones than are really needed. As triad arrange-

	Wт			Wт	
R	Y	B	R	Y	B
VR	OY	GB	RO	YG	BV
V	O	G	O	G	V
BV	RO	YG	OY	GB	VR
B	R	Y	Y	B	R
GB	VR	OY	YG	BV	RO
G	V	O	G	V	O
	Blk			Blk	

Fig. 60.   Type B Palettes — Triads.

ments are usually the best for ordinary purposes in Type A scales, so the complementary pair arrangements are usually the more satisfactory in Type B scales.

Variations in Arrangement and Use of Scaled Palettes

No matter how scales may be worked out, so long as they have definite order in them, they will be found to fall into one of these main classes, called here Type A and Type B respectively; and in each of these main types complementary pairs and triads will be found the most useful and the most usual arrangements. The exact intervals between values and between colors may, as pointed out above, be varied indefinitely.

In all the scales described in the preceding pages, the tones within each value register are all

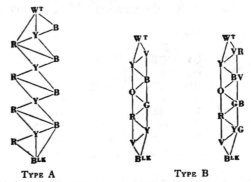

TYPE A   TYPE B

FIG. 61.   Palettes with a Sequence of Values in each Register.

NOTE: Mixtures on the palette would naturally be confined to those indicated by the connecting lines.

placed at the same value; but a sequence of values might be established in each register, as in fig. 61. An arrangement of this sort is especially advantageous, if the scale is composed of only a few registers. It may be convenient at times to arrange the tones on the palette in a single column, as in fig. 62. The general character of the scale is not changed by so doing.

The definite use of scales in actual painting cannot ordinarily be learned without some personal instruction; but in general it may be stated that the tones, having once been fixed on the palette, may be mixed on the palette, or they may be mixed entirely on the canvas, or they may be juxtaposed on the canvas practically

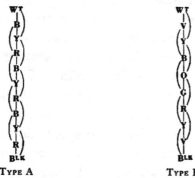

TYPE A   TYPE B

FIG. 62. Palettes with Tones Arranged in a Single Column.

without mixing, as in well-established practices of handling. It is better, however, to mix as little as possible on the palette, for intimate mixing is likely to lower the value below that of the tones mixed, especially if high intensities are employed. An experienced painter will ordinarily mix his tones to a large extent on his brush, picking up the right amount of adjacent tones so that the stroke, without producing an intimate mixture,

137

will give the tone required. Refinements may be achieved by overlaying or interknitting of strokes in the wet paint without destroying the freshness of quality. One matter to which few painters at the present day pay sufficient attention is the necessity for uniform handling over the whole surface of a painting. This is a most important consideration, for, unless the details in all parts of the composition are handled with the same degree of minuteness, there will be a distinct feeling of inharmonious scale of handling in the composition as a whole. The handling may be broad, or it may be fine; it must be uniform or it must be varied according to some definite system of focus. It should not be minute in one place and broad in another without definite reason; it should not be hard edged in one part and soft edged in others. Almost all of the French and Italian paintings of the xviii century are notable for their harmonious scale of handling. Even the skies or flat wall surfaces are painted in such a way that there is in them a feeling of the same measure of touch as in the modelling of a face or in the indication of the texture of a lace collar.

One great advantage in the use of scaled palettes is that a painter may think out the whole

tone arrangement of his work before starting to
paint, and may then execute the various fields
independently, working steadily from day to
day, without the necessity of final retouching.
Moreover, a painter may think out his work in
such a way that he may easily paint from imagination or on the basis of drawings made from
nature. A portrait may be painted on the basis
of a drawing made at perhaps only one sitting,
without the necessity for further sittings, in the
manner followed by Holbein and other painters
of the Renaissance. Notes in regard to the various local tones, like those made by Holbein, as
an aid to the memory, are all that is required.
On the basis of such a definite procedure, fresh
and uniform quality of surface may be achieved
over a whole composition. This was very much
the regular procedure followed by all painters
down to the close of the xviii century, and this
accounts for the difference in quality between
the work of even a minor painter before the end
of the xviii century and the typical work even
of the greatest men of the xix century. Muddy-
ing of quality results necessarily from the usual
practice in vogue at the present day of approxi-
mating the main masses of a composition over
the whole surface, and then correcting and re-

working in endless repainting over the top. No painting can be satisfactory in quality unless every stroke from the canvas up is in its right place, calculated to play its proper part in the final effect. The modern painter can ordinarily achieve fresh quality only in a quick sketch.

USE OF SCALED PALETTES IN THE RENAISSANCE

That the masters of the Renaissance used palettes which were carefully arranged in something of the manner of the more precisely scaled palettes discussed above, may be observed by a careful examination of their works; but on account of the overlaying and mixing of tones in the final painting, it is usually impossible to tell exactly what all the original tones on the palette may have been, or exactly how they were used, though at times it is probably possible to come surprisingly close to it. Usually, when artists or other persons came to write about painting, they found it too difficult to describe their technical procedures in words, — partly, no doubt, because they had no definite terms for the different factors that enter into tone, — and, although frequently discussing pigment materials and their preparation in detail, they were apt to pass over the far more important part of the subject,

which refers to the laying-out of the palette and
the way in which the tones prepared thereon
were mixed and applied in actual painting, with
the remark that this could be learned only by
practice under a master. Occasionally, however,
writers have attempted to give more detailed
information in regard to the way in which pigments were laid out on the palette, or arranged
in vases, as in painting in fresco and tempera,
and how these were used in practice. As at the
present day we unfortunately have no masters,
at least in the sense in which those of the Renaissance were masters, these accounts are of the
greatest interest in supplementing the information which we may obtain from the paintings
themselves.

Of all these accounts that of Cennino Cennini [1] is the fullest and in many ways the most
important; but the procedures which he describes are those of xiv and xv century fresco
and tempera painters, and these cannot be applied directly to painting at the present day, unless it is very archaistic in style. There are also
fragmentary accounts of later Renaissance procedures in certain books written in the xvii and
xviii centuries. So far, however, investigators

[1] *Op. cit.*

in going through these documents have confined their attention almost exclusively to the question of pigment materials and media, or else to general aesthetic questions about which the XVII and XVIII century artists did such a lot of inconclusive talking and writing. A careful search of documents of the later Renaissance from the point of view of scaled palettes might be most instructive.[1] One or two passages such as I have in mind will be referred to presently.

In the painting of the Middle Ages and the earlier Renaissance a distinct scale was usually employed for each of the separate fields of the composition. Cennino describes very clearly how this was done in the XIV century. A red drapery, for example, was painted by preparing three main tones for the three main planes of light, half-light, and shadow: red with a very small touch of white for the shadow, more white for the half-light, and still more white for the light. The value and intensity relations of this scale are shown in fig. 21. White, or white with a little red, would be used for a few touches of high light, and red alone, or with a little black, for a few accents of deep shadow. The highest inten-

[1] Much interesting material has been gathered together in the book on *La couleur* in the series called L'art enseigné par les maîtres, by Henri Guerlin. Henri Laurens, Paris.

sity of color came in the shadow. Draperies of
blue or of other colors were painted in a similar
manner. Flesh was painted in a combination of
different values of red, or red-orange, and green
or yellow-green. This procedure described by
Cennino continued in use in much of the Italian
painting of the xv and even of the xvi century.
Sometimes, however, it was varied. Yellow, instead of white, was sometimes used to produce
the lighter tones in painting a drapery, producing in the case of the reddish drapery a sequence
of color from R in shadow, to O or RO in half-
light, to Y or OY in the light. In another drapery,
the sequence of color might be from B in shadow,
to GB or G in half-light, to YG or Y in the light.
Sequences of color of this sort are to be found
also in Byzantine mosaics, and in tapestries and
embroideries of the Renaissance. They might be
classed as Type B scales.

The painters of the xvi and xvii centuries
continued to handle their separate fields almost
independently, but there seems to be little written record of the procedures of this time. In
Venetian painting of the xvi century, a system
of opaque underpainting, with superposed transparent glazes, was used. For the flesh, the underpainting was apparently often executed entirely

in white, black, and red, — the same limited
range of color as shown in scale J in fig. 51,
— and over this opaque foundation might sometimes be passed a glaze of yellow, with perhaps
some small preliminary touches of transparent
red. Other tones were obtained by means of
glazes over the underpainting, or by variations
in the tone of the underpainting.[1] Simple opaque
underpaintings with superposed glazes in the
manner of Venetian painting were used exten-
sively in the later Renaissance. The work of Lely
illustrates this method especially clearly. Sometimes, especially for cool colors, the underpainting was apparently simply neutral, in mixtures
of white and black pigments, with glazes of blue
or green above. Gradually, however, painters
came to lay out their whole palettes in an arrangement of tones which, with slight variations
and a certain amount of glazing, could be used as
a basis for the painting of all the different fields
of a composition. This may be seen in the work
of Rubens, and more especially in that of painters of the XVIII century, like Tiepolo or Bou-

[1] In the work of Titian, Tintoretto, and Veronese, toward the
end of the XVI century, there was often a building-up of the
final effect in an alternation of scumbling (opaque light over
dark) and glazing, that was as far removed as possible from any
imitative procedure.

cher, who constantly used palettes in red, yellow, and blue, similar to that shown in scale A in fig. 50, but with an extra column of neutrals with which the different colors would ordinarily be mixed. Some writers of the XVIII century speak of the necessity of having a picture appear as if it were all painted with a single palette.[1]

A description of what is probably a typical XVII century palette I have found in a book called *Les premiers éléments de la peinture pratique*, by J. B. Corneille, Peintre de l'Académie Royale, published in 1684. This palette is one arranged especially for painting a head, but Corneille explains that other fields are to be painted in a similar manner. A simple set of pigments is arranged along the outer edge of the

---

[1] "Les couleurs doivent avoir quelque correspondance entr'elles, une perpetuelle union, les unes avec les autres, ce qu'on appelle aussi l'entente des couleurs; c'est pourquoi l'on dit qu'il faudrait qu'un Tableau fut peint d'une seule Palette." (*Traité sur la peinture*, par Me. Bernard du Puy du Grez, 1700.)

"M. Jouvenet portait souvent la couleur de ses chairs pour rompre ses draperies et pour les accorder ensemble; cela revient à l'unisson et produit en partie les effets dont je viens de parler. Il est certain que si toutes ces couleurs participent les unes des autres, il est impossible qu'il n'y ait de l'union; car le participation des couleurs contribue beaucoup à l'harmonie d'un tableau, et je pense que c'est ce qui fait dire des tableaux harmonieux qu'ils semble avoir été faits d'une seule palette." (*Essai sur les principes de la peinture*, par Jean Restout, peintre ordinaire du roi, Louis XV; publié avec des notes par A.-R. R. de Formigny de la Londe. Caen, 1863.)

palette, beginning with the lighter ones near the thumb-hole and ending with the darker ones farther away at the left end of the palette. On the main part of the palette are then mixed up two sets of tones, one called "jours," the other "demi-teintes" and "ombres," to correspond roughly to the warmer tones of the lights and the cooler tones of the half-lights and shadows. As a matter of fact the arrangement results in two parallel columns with five values in each column, the lighter tones placed at the right nearest the thumb, grading down to darker tones at the left. One column consists of different values of red, made of mixtures of white with vermilion and lake in varying proportions; a light yellow, made of yellow ochre and white, is placed at the extreme right for the highest lights. The other column consists of a series of neutral tones of varying values, grading down almost to black; they are made of mixtures of red, yellow, and blue (or black in place of the blue) pigments, with white used in varying amounts in the lighter ones. These two columns form the basis for the painting; but other pigments are placed at the side to be used in connection with the other tones. The arrangement of the main part of the palette, but turned into a vertical position,

is shown in fig. 63. Supplementary tones of varying values and colors were mixed up on the
palette, but great emphasis is placed, in this as
in other books, on the necessity of keeping the
paint as fresh as possible, the subtler mixtures
being made as far as possible by juxtaposing
tones on the brush and leaving them undisturbed
when applied to the canvas.

```
                        Wт
                         Y
                   R
                   R        N
        RO         R    Y   N
        (Vermilion) R       N    B
        R                   N
        (Lake)              N
                   Blk
```

Fig. 63. The Palette Described by Corneille in 1684.

All this bears testimony to an extremely careful preparation of the tones on the palette; and
all through the xviii century and into the xix
century, painters continued to prepare their palettes in this painstaking way, as long as the
workshop tradition lasted. The final loss of this
tradition was due partly to the fact that painters, as well as the general public, which in the
course of the xix century developed into an
extensive but undiscriminating patron and critic
of the arts, became obsessed with the idea of

147

imitation as the end of all art; partly to the supplanting of the older manner of training the artist as an apprentice in the workshop of a master, with the modern art-school training. In France, the break came rather suddenly with the suppression of the old French academy by David. It must be remembered that the old academy of the XVII and XVIII centuries was very different from the modern academy. It was more like a mediaeval guild. Formal instruction in the academy was confined to drawing and occasional lectures. The practice of painting was learned in the workshop of the master as in the earlier Renaissance. The academy stood for tradition, at times somewhat narrow, no doubt, but nevertheless almost indispensable, unless something can be found to take its place. Some, at any rate, of the advantages of that tradition may be recovered by a rational education of the artist in a thorough understanding of the limitations and the possibilities of the terms by means of which he must express his ideas, and of the general principles which govern their use.

APPENDIX

APPENDIX

THE EMOTIONAL SIGNIFICANCE OF DIF-
FERENT GENERAL TONALITIES

A DISCUSSION of the general subject of color would
hardly be complete without some reference to the
emotional significance of varying tonalities, or of
varying arrangements of tone contrasts. This has to
do especially with the possibilities of expression of
mood by the deliberate choice of certain ranges of
colors, color-intensities, or values, or by strong or
slight contrasts of any of these factors, aside from
the matter of arrangement from the standpoint of
formal design. It is a matter of common experience
that on the stage a yellowish tonality suggests an atmosphere of general cheerfulness, as opposed to the
feeling of gloominess often produced by a subdued
violetish lighting. Psychologists have conducted experiments to test the emotional reaction to different
colored lighting effects, and red has naturally been
found exciting, yellow on the whole more cheerful,
green restful, and violets and violet-blues comparatively depressing. The ranges of values and of intensities, as well as of color, would in this case play a
part in the general effect. The emotional result is
partly a matter of association, but partly also, I suppose, a matter of definite physiological reaction.
Many of these variations in reaction to different
tonalities seem to be fairly universal, and they may
be used to enhance the expression of general mood
in painting or in lighting on the stage. Variations
in the strength of contrast between the tones in

a composition may also have an emotional significance. A more exciting effect is produced by sharply
defined contrasts from tone to tone, a more restful
effect by gradual transitions. Similar differences of
effect may be produced by a breaking-up of the
measures of the tones to produce a choppy, lively
effect, as opposed to the greater calm and dignity to
be obtained in juxtaposition of large and simple
masses. The tonal arrangements of a composition
may thus be made to emphasize the character of the
general conception.

The possibilities of expression suggested above
have been used more or less definitely in a great deal
of the painting of the past; but in the last few years
they have been pushed farther, I believe, in connection with design and lighting on the stage than in
painting. The emotional effects of the tone in recent
so-called expressionistic paintings seem often to have
been accidental, rather than planned deliberately.
One of the most obvious illustrations of the suggestion of definite mood to be obtained by the use of
different colored tonalities which have come to my
attention was in some painted designs done by Boris
Anisfeld for sets for the *Arabian Nights* and *Les
Sylphides*. As compared with the hot and stuffy
orange tonality in the design for the *Arabian Nights*,
a yellow-greenish effect in the other ballet was perfectly definite in its differentiation of mood. Examples of definite expression by variation of contrast
and mass may be found in much of the painting of
the Renaissance, and also occasional differentiations
of general tonality that are effective in the suggestion
of changing mood. As far as I know, the subject has

not been very thoroughly studied either in connection with the painting of the past or as to its theoretical possibilities.

THE QUESTION OF PREFERENCE FOR INDIVIDUAL TONES

INVESTIGATIONS have sometimes been conducted in which large numbers of persons have been asked to express their relative preference or dislike for a series of individual tones. It has always seemed to me that in connection with the problem of aesthetic experience the results of these investigations are of little significance, even if it could be shown that they were fairly universal and based on physiological reactions. As a matter of fact many of our simple preferences are founded on merely personal association and prejudice, and, although it may be true that we cannot enjoy very much looking at anything which we associate with a disagreeable event or with a person whom we dislike, still mere agreeableness has little to do with aesthetic experience, except as a possible condition. Ordinary likes and dislikes are transcended by the organization that underlies aesthetic experience of the higher orders. It is possible that popular art, with its short-lived appeal, can hardly afford to be disagreeable, — we must have our pretty faces and our happy endings, — but art of more lasting value may often be based on motives which are in themselves not at all pleasant. Examples in music and literature will readily occur to anyone. In tone relations in painting the harmony resulting from a definite organization of relationships is of much greater importance than the superficial attractiveness of this or that individual tone. Many persons have what they call their favorite colors or colors which they dislike. Often this depends primarily on what is thought to be becoming to a particular complexion, or on some individual association or experience. Sometimes a prejudice of this sort may be well-nigh universal in a given community for a certain time. Thus in the xix century people were not used to seeing violet tones used very much in painting, and at first they tended to dislike all pictures in which intense violets appeared, or in fact high intensities of any colors. The dislike for violet arose partly from the fact that violet tonality in a picture was apt to be out of harmony with the usual decorative surroundings of the xix century, but it was due largely to unthinking prejudice. To-day we have almost all of us got over our dislike for violetish tones and high intensities in general, when properly used. Sentimental people and those who like to pose as being "artistic" are, of course, apt to pride themselves on their individual preferences, and no doubt our personal leanings by their variety add somewhat to the gayety of life; but, as a general rule, an intelligent person may, if he likes, get over his prejudices in regard to particular colors or tonalities, as he may frequently surmount other prejudices of association which interfere with aesthetic judgment and artistic appreciation.

BIBLIOGRAPHICAL NOTE

A selected list of some of the more important books and articles which may be found useful in connection with the subject-matter of this book is given below; but it must be understood that there is no intention to make this anything like a complete bibliography.

For the general theory of color vision the reader may be referred to the following books:

Troland, L. T. (Chairman), "Report of the Colorimetry Committee of the Optical Society of America, 1920–21," *Journal of the Optical Society of America*, vol. VI, No. 6 (August, 1922).

Parsons, Sir J. H., *An Introduction to the Study of Colour Vision* (second edition). Cambridge University Press, 1924.

Ladd-Franklin, C., *Colour and Colour Theories*. Harcourt, Brace and Company, New York, 1929.

Reiser, O. L., *The Alchemy of Light and Color*. W. W. Norton and Company, New York, 1928.

Luckiesh, M., *Color and its Applications*. D. Van Nostrand Company, New York, 1915.

Martin, L. C., and Gamble, W., *Colour and Methods of Colour Reproduction*. D. Van Nostrand Company, New York, 1923.

Rood, O. N., *Modern Chromatics*. D. Appleton and Company, New York, 1879.

Ames, A., Jr., "Systems of Color Standards," *Journal of the Optical Society of America*, vol. V, No. 2 (March, 1921).

In addition to these, mention should be made of Professor L. T. Troland's book entitled *The Principles of Psy-*

chophysiology, which is to be published in the near future.

For discussions of various systems of classification and nomenclature, the following books will be found particularly useful:

Munsell, A. H., *A Color Notation*. G. H. Ellis Company, Boston, 1905.

——, *Atlas of the Munsell Color System*. Now published by the Munsell Research Laboratory, Baltimore.

The Munsell classification is unquestionably the most accurate, and the most useful for mechanical purposes, that has yet been devised For the purposes of the painter, however, it does not work as well as the more approximate classification devised by Dr. Ross and set forth in the present book in the form of a working tone solid and diagrams derived therefrom. A defect in the proportions of the Munsell solid is discussed in the text.

Ridgway, R., *Color Standards and Color Nomenclature*. Washington, D. C., 1912.

This was prepared especially for the use of botanists. It is defective in its use of a different set of value levels and intervals for each hue.

Ruxton's Color System. Philip Ruxton, Inc., New York, 1910.

This was prepared especially for the use of printers. It is based on a system of classification by saturation and brightness, as I have defined these terms; but it is not very accurate and has, I am told, gone out of use as too cumbersome.

Andrews, E. C., *Color and its Application to Printing*. The Inland Printer Company, Chicago, 1911.

This is based on the Munsell classification.

The books given below deal more particularly with the art of painting:

Ross, D. W., *A Theory of Pure Design*. Houghton Mifflin Company, Boston, 1907.

——, *On Drawing and Painting*. Houghton Mifflin Company, Boston, 1912.

BIBLIOGRAPHICAL NOTE

Ross, D. W., *The Painter's Palette*. Houghton Mifflin Company, Boston, 1919.

Sargent, Walter, *The Enjoyment and Use of Color*. Charles Scribner's Sons, New York, 1923.

Cutler, C. G., and Pepper, S. C., *Modern Color*. Harvard University Press, Cambridge, 1923.

Reference to other books will be found in the text.

PLATES

NOTE

The following plates are *approximate* renderings of certain of the charts which are illustrated by abstract diagrams in the body of the book. *They are not to be regarded as standards of measure.* In the three-color process in half-tone used in these plates, in spite of painstaking correction on the part of the engraver, it is impossible to approach with more than moderate closeness to the tones of the original charts, which are executed in a variety of pigments in water-color. The plates will serve their purpose if they enable the reader, who is not actually making the charts for himself, to obtain a somewhat more definite idea of the distinction between the different factors in tone discussed in the text.

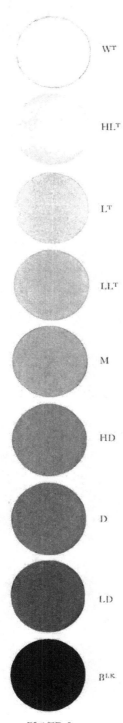

WT

HLT

LT

LLT

M

HD

D

LD

BLK.

PLATE I

THE SCALE OF VALUES

(Compare with fig. 1)

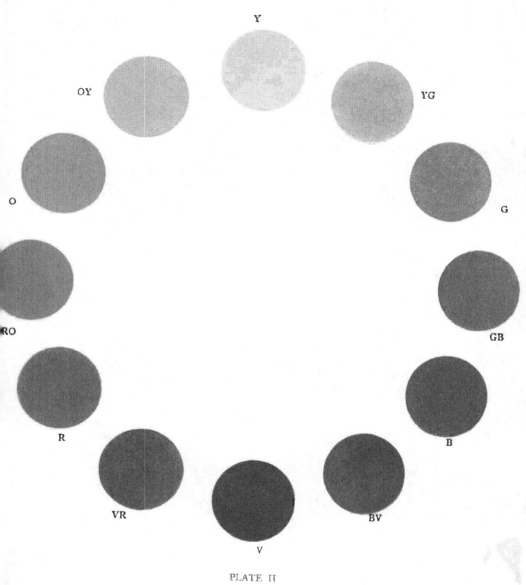

PLATE II

THE SCALE OF COLORS

(Compare with fig. 2)

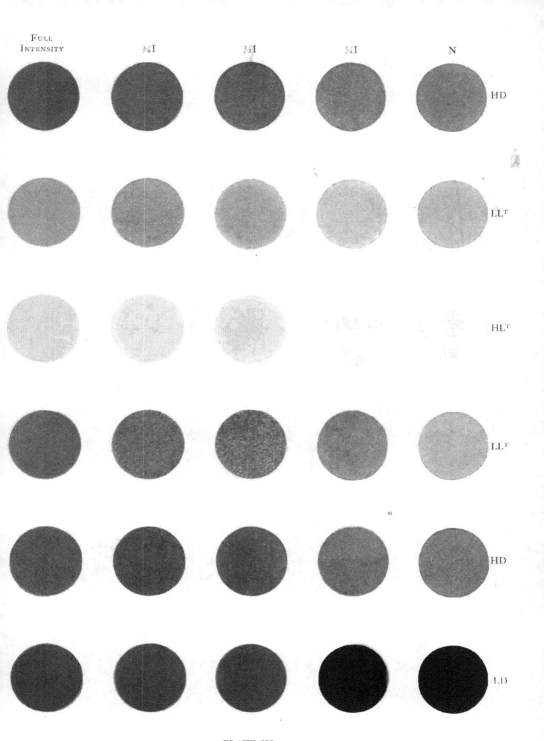

PLATE III

THE SCALE OF INTENSITIES FOR
SIX PRINCIPAL COLORS
(Compare with fig. 3)

Full Intensity	$\frac{3}{4}$I	$\frac{1}{2}$I	$\frac{1}{4}$I	N	
					W^T
					HL^T
					L^T
					LL^T
					M
					HD
					D
					LD
					B^{LK}

PLATE IV

THE VALUE AND INTENSITY POSSIBILITIES OF THE
SINGLE COLOR RED–ORANGE

(Compare with fig. 7)

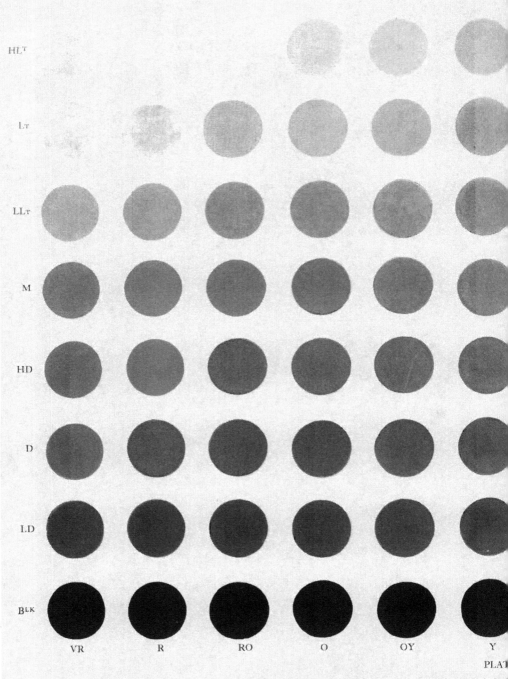

THE HIGHEST INTENSITIES OF THE TWELVE CO
BETWEEN BLAC

(This corresponds to fig. 11, except that the column o

YG G GB B BV V

AT THE SEVEN DIFFERENT VALUE LEVELS
ND WHITE

is here placed at the left instead of at the right)